From

The Women's Press Ltd
124 Shoreditch High Street, London E1

Padma Perera · *Photo by Fleur Weymouth*

Padma Perera, who has also written under the name of Padma Hejmadi, was born in Madras and educated in India and at the University of Michigan, Ann Arbor. While at Michigan she won the Hopwood Award for fiction, and since then has received a number of fellowships for her writing. She has given readings and seminars at Vassar, Columbia University, the Rhode Island School of Design, etc., and taught for some years at the University of Colorado, Boulder. She has been an Indian dancer of the classical Manipuri style, she has a book on dance 'brewing', and another on traditional handicrafts.

In addition to *Birthday Deathday*, Padma Perera has had two collections of short stories published in USA and India (*Coigns of Vantage*, 1978) as well as a work of non-fiction, *The Challenge of Indian Fiction in English*, 1975. Her essays and stories have appeared in *The New Yorker*, *The Saturday Evening Post*, *Horizon*, *The Iowa Review* and elsewhere.

She is presently collaborating with her sister Sumana Chandavarkar to translate the poetry of the fifteenth-century Hindi poet Mira Bai, for a song cycle by composer Laura Clayton.

PADMA PERERA

Birthday Deathday
and Other Stories

The Women's Press

First published in Great Britain by
The Women's Press Limited 1985
A member of the Namara Group
124 Shoreditch High Street, London E1 6JE

The first nine stories in this collection were published as *Dr Salaam & Other Stories of India* by the Capra Press, California, 1978; 'Spaces of Decision' in *Helicon Nine*, Winter 1982; and 'Afternoon of the House' in *The New Yorker*, June 1974

British Library Cataloguing in Publication Data

Perera, Padma
  Birthday deathday.
  I. Title
  823[F]   PR9499.3.P41

  ISBN 0-7043-2874-7
  ISBN 0-7043-3984-6 Pbk

  Printed and bound in Great Britain by Nene Litho and Woolnough Bookbinding both of Irthlingborough, Northants

For Nandita, Raj, Ahalya, Shanta

Contents

Acknowledgements

The following stories appeared originally in *The New Yorker*: 'The Schoolmaster,' 'Too Late for Anger,' 'Doctor Salaam,' 'Mauna,' and 'Afternoon of the House'. 'Spaces of Decision: 1890s–1970s' was published in *Helicon Nine, A Journal of Women's Arts and Letters*; 'Eknath,' and 'Birthday Deathday' in *The Southern Review*; and 'Appa-mam' and 'Monologue for Foreigners' in *The Illustrated Weekly of India*. The translation from the Bhagavad Gita on page 000 is by Christopher Isherwood and Swami Prabhavananda.

The author wishes to express her gratitude to The McDowell Colony, Peterborough, New Hampshire, and to the Helene Wurlitzer Foundation of New Mexico, Taos, New Mexico, where some of these stories were written.

Loving thanks to Raghvir and Vrinda Kumble for being such a source of sustenance. And as always, a special and deep appreciation of my parents, Rukma and Vasudev Hejmadi – who have been dedicated-to, over and over, so I spare them this time.

Birthday Deathday

For a long time the train circles the town, defining it, as a dog will circle a patch of ground to mark his sleeping place. As other journeys have circled their destination – Innsbruck, two years ago; the bus from Venice reaching a cup of hills and then slowly rounding its rim in the darkness, descending tier by smaller tier to a handful of jewels glimmering at the bottom of the valley. 'Innsbruck!' the driver cried when the jewels became street lights: a destination reached. 'Innsbruck – !' springing out on Austrian soil and at once becoming aggressively Italian, pushing the blue cap to the back of his head, tired but tirelessly male and appreciative, eyeing each woman passenger as she stepped out pale and blinking a little, dizzy from circling the hills.

As I have circled decisions, hesitating on the brink of commitment: what is this, before I embrace it? But I cannot know until I've embraced it. As I could not identify the jewels until they turned into Innsbruck, nor can really assimilate this dusty Deccan town, last seen five years ago, until I return again today. Is this the measure of age then? – not chronology but layers of awareness: the remembering, the likening, the overlap of experience. I am not twenty-five but two similar journeys to be encompassed and understood.

'Excuse me, shall I pull down that window for you?' The man across. Unctuous. Fatly solicitous.

'No, thank you.' Take notes to share with your sister: a profiteer, what else? Bet he bribed the booking clerk to get a lower berth. Will she say that or will you? Being with her is a perpetual *déjà vu*: everything felt is repeated; everything known is deepened and returned by her quality as by time.

'But you are facing the engine, isn't it? You may be getting coal in your eye.'

'No, no. I'm all right. Really. Don't bother, it's very kind of you.' Kind indeed, when scarcely half an hour has elapsed since he

1

bullied his secretary so unmercifully at the last station! Such misplaced and heavy-handed chivalry. Probably beats his wife. Look studiedly out at the dark earth slipping past: black-cotton-soil-of-the-Central-Indian-plateau . . . At what point did that cease being a textbook phrase and become landscape seen from moving windows? Why, when a trip grows from ambition to actuality, does it at once change its shape? Poring over atlases as a child, tracing routes with a grubby forefinger: I want to go there and there and there. See that and that and that. When first did 'there' and 'that' get tinged with 'them' – a place endued with persons met, an alien landscape made unalterably yours because you caught a cold there or ran into a friend at the corner or were so desperately unhappy that in acknowledging your misery you accepted its surroundings as well?

Neither colds nor griefs nor friendships in Innsbruck, yet a journey out as jewelled as the journey in: to my tropical eyes the very first glimpse of springtime in a temperate climate – such new and tender green light everywhere, everywhere, everywhere, until the whole world had turned to emerald. Here the ground is black and baked; the sun beats down. No, the journeys are not similar after all. There in Europe the circles were described in depth, feasting the eyes and the senses. Here in India these train tracks draw horizontal rings around the town while the town itself stands deep with age and implication, casually shuffling the centuries together as if they were a well-thumbed pack of cards.

Remember writing about that to my husband last time, five years ago, when he was still merely a friend and a foreigner, adding: 'You must come here, you simply must.' And now he will . . . and now he will. . . . Train wheels take up the rhythm, toss it irrepressibly along. I dare not smile, the man across may smile back and start making overtures again. With a violent lurch the tempo slows down: . . . and . . . now . . . he . . . will. Why are they stopping? Have we arrived already?

'No signal probably,' the man says.

Nothing outside but the hot blue immensity of sky; fields lying fallow; a single bullock-cart propped forward on its shafts, the bull disengaged and tethered to a stump close by, the driver snoozing in the shade of a scraggly babul tree. Clusters of huts in the distance: dried thatch, mud walls, black earth. Suddenly out of nowhere a beggar woman comes – thin, of no age at all, hair pulled back into a peasant knot, protruding teeth, a baby asleep on her shoulder. She has covered its head with the tattered end of her sari; beneath it escape stick-like arms and legs. I open my purse and find a coin.

'You should wait until we are about to start and *then* give,' says the man. 'Now, see, they'll all come running.'

In place of the woman a boy of less than three. Faded blue shirt barely covering his belly; around his hips a thin black cord against the evil eye; his sex, spindly thighs and feet stained with dust and urine; one eye a running sore on which flies settle and do not fly away. He doesn't raise his hand to ward them off, he just extends it, palm upward: 'Amma . . .'

'You are simply encouraging them. This is how even able-bodied fellows become beggars.' (Echoes of a cartoon in a Madras newspaper: one wayside beggar informing another: 'I have decided to open a branch office.') An old man now, a girl, a cripple, two more men – 'See what I told you? Able-bodied chaps.'

No more coins left, no change to pay the porter when I get off. Suddenly I am afraid: of vultures gathering, of the fattest vulture of them all in front of me, drawing up a bulging *dhoti*-clad leg to lean back more comfortably against the buttoned upholstery. The train gives a warning lurch. Calmly he feels in his pocket, opens a shiny wallet and, shaking out a few coins, flings them from the window just as we begin to move. The beggars scatter and then avidly converge, getting down on their hands and knees, scrounging in the dust; left behind. Wheels rattle louder, spin faster, devouring every hunger and shame and platitutde: *If you give to one, they all come running. Whatever you do is a drop in the ocean* . . . The man belches, complacent. His point has been proven, his vanity fed.

Abroad, in Europe and America, I've chafed against the stuffy impersonality of trains: hermetically sealed off from outside smells and sounds, neatly dispensing with even their own thudding clatter as they glide in and out of dumb-show stations. Here one is thrown open with every window to every scrap and pain of life. To shut out, to soft-pedal, is to be lessened: not so lacerated, not so responsible, that much less alive. Profiteers are part of the bargain then – will this trip never end?

All of a sudden it does. Against the sliding blur of people and noise – red turbans of the coolies, cries of the platform vendors, bookstalls, piles of luggage, cavernous waiting rooms – a vivid delicate face springs into focus, eagerly scanning each compartment as it rumbles by. My sister. Thin hand, replica of my own, clasps

3

mine. We have never looked alike, only hands to show the comforting kinship.

'How was it?'

'All right.' Tell her later.

Jostling of people, manoeuvring of luggage. 'Suitcase, bedding, water-jug. Nothing else? Sure?'

'Sure. Oh, and I've no change.'

'What did you do, eat it? Never mind, I have enough.'

Incredible how anyone so exquisite can be so efficient. To avoid the last-minute scramble she has engaged a porter well ahead of time. Number 83 on his brass badge; but by now, especially with the train so late, she must have divined not only his name but that of his wife, his children, his village and his sure-fire remedy for whooping cough. He coils his turban into a cushion padding the crown of his head, places the suitcase on top of it, swings up the bed-roll in a single gesture and strides off toward the exit. Holding the heavy earthen water-jug between us, we try to follow, only to be blocked off at every second step by what seems to be a welcoming committee of sorts thronging my fellow traveller. Flashbulbs pop and sizzle against an overpowering odour of roses and human sweat. Can't point him out to my sister, he is hidden by the crowds, unseen but well imagined: laden with garlands and the lard of his own importance. In a sudden access of distaste I lose my bearings. 'Hey, where did our porter go?'

'Jeevanlal? He said he'd wait for us at the gate – what are you giggling at?'

Your knowing his name. Reaffirmation of faith and familiarity. Sheer giddy relief that, for once, those whom I most cherish will be safe within the bounds of a single country, not scattered haphazard across the globe to turn travel from a luxury to a life-line.

Answering my thoughts, she tells me the moment we escape the clamour of the platform: 'Guess whose cable we got today?'

My turn to beg. 'He's coming soon?'

'Day after tomorrow. The visa has come through. He wired to say he'd grab the earliest available flight out.'

Never has this town been more layered with time, personal time now, three layers on every dust mote: the future of his arrival day after tomorrow; the actuality of our presence here today; and over it all the remnants of the past, five years ago: a sense of reading over my own forgotten shoulder, therefore, able to wander in the garden or write letters while the elders talked, shown the town as now I can

4

show my sister.

'We haven't been together on a trip like this since high school, do you realize that?'

But she doesn't hear me, busy settling accounts with Jeevanlal and wearing her absorbed, practical face so absurdly resembling her three-year-old son's that I in turn am distracted and do not hear when she speaks.

'Psst! Snap out of it. I said taxi or tonga?'

'Tonga, of course.' Remember to tell him this when he arrives: as children, out in the districts, down endless country roads edged with rice fields, we went to elementary school in a tonga painted bright blue, the horse stepping smartly along in feathered crest and jingling harness, the driver whistling film songs to its beat.

Today our driver is mournful, with drooping moustaches and a dispirited horse called Raja. When he says 'Ai, Raja, ai!' and flourishes his whip, it livens tentatively up to a trot, only to lapse back soon enough to its habitual shuffle.

'Leave him be,' my sister says. 'We are in no hurry. Is he an old horse?'

'Old? *Raja*? Why, I got him scarcely a month ago at the very best age a horse can be –' Moustaches bristle; he is lying and they both know it, a companionable feeling.

She asks him where he lives, he tells her; talks of his brother, a tenant farmer; the monsoons; the crops; a new dam being built upriver . . . See it again: her inheritance, as firstborn, of our parents' gift: of giving themselves so simply to the substance of things while never losing their own complexity, so that every human encounter is allowed to fill its limits, whether rounded and complete or probing jagged corners; in accord or in argument, always that sense of a touchstone.

Easy to think, away from them: 'It couldn't be. Distance does it. I'm idealizing,' only to come home and be witness again, watching her now, wondering: When did envy of her as a sister stop and delight in her as a person begin? Past how many childhood resentments, absences, miles, years, growing up parallel though separate to reach this spacious closeness – a ripening result of time, once more, as only this dusty town can evoke it.

'When did you arrive?'

'Yesterday.'

'How are our host and hostess?'

Eyes solemnly widen. 'They are away today, but you can

5

imagine.'

'Yes, I can.' I start giggling again. Between us they are a private joke with all the probable improbability of a cartoon: Highly respected literati from a wealthy business clan who have set themselves up as patrons of the arts and the sciences alike, benignly engrossed in charities, ideally engrossed in each other – perfect couple, share and share alike: he takes on the sciences while she appropriates the arts. Regularly over the years they have also brought up innumerable nieces and nephews, sheltered destitute cousins and widowed great-aunts, finally becoming, though childless themselves, titular heads of a huge and constantly accruing household. Why then should their laudable lives give off such a tinny sound?

'Perhaps,' my sister suggests thoughtfully, 'because they seem to stake such proprietary claim on all compassion and conjugal bliss . . . Nobody can expect to get away with that, now can they?' Chin in hand, as we jog up and down, she watches the road unrolling like a broad grey ribbon beneath the tonga wheels, skirting bazaar and cantonment area to take us to the oldest quarter of town beyond the university campus. 'I was thinking about it when I woke up today. Lay in bed waggling my foot and listening to all the early-morning sounds around their place – cook yelling, taps running, old lady brushing her teeth with a neem-twig and making such alarming noises in the process that –'

'Good God!' At my groan, so loud and unexpected, the tonga driver turns around to glance speculatively at us above his moustaches. 'Don't tell me *she's* there now.'

'Where else would she be, poor thing? And they've never harboured an international marriage in the house before, so you might as well prepare yourself for an inquisition.'

Dismaying prospect. The old lady, our hostess's aunt, is like no other old lady we know: possessed and personified by a curiosity so all-consuming that she has passed into a proverb in our dialect – eternally she lifts lids to peek beneath, opens doors to hear within, tweaks the curtains in every bedroom to flush out some possibly lurking lover. . . . Yet now in the old house she stands like a painting under the high shadowy arches of the verandah: deep red sari offsetting white walls, grey stone floors; a waiting, parched-ivory face, deceptively bland and fine-boned.

'Why are you so late? How much did you pay the tonga? How many hours did you spend on the train? Were you alone in the compartment? Did anyone try to molest you? Why hasn't your husband come with you, have you quarrelled? Oh, will the visa be ready by the time he leaves? Is this why you and he and your sister are coming from three different directions on three different days instead of travelling together like sensible people? Where will you go next? Where are your parents now? How long . . .?'

Age. This too, ceaseless reckoning of people and places and times, usually dismissed in formula: Curiosity Keeps Her Alive. Or could it perhaps have been congenital in her case? Once to be deplored, now accepted and even indulged. With so little of it left, she is entitled to leaven her life as she chooses. ('Crowded as our conditions are, we can have room and respect for our old people.' Who said that, so righteous and resonant? Politician? Poet? Someone in a dream?) So now she welcomes visitors, fusses over the younger generation –' The boys are in Darjeeling, the girls are down south.'

Can't get a word in edgewise to ask what boys? Which girls? No matter. For the moment, a house blessedly empty and beautiful. Curtains from Orissa, handwoven and the colour of wet earth. Kashmiri rugs on the floor – mountain and cloud, kingfisher and chenar leaf, against the cool grey stone. A Tibetan prayer wheel. Tanjore bronzes. On one entire wall a great carved lintel from a South Indian temple. Objects disparate yet coherent like the landscapes they represent, blown together by the wind through open doors, held together by the spaces in the old house, intact as when a spendthrift Nawab built it fifteen generations ago.

'Lovely,' I admit *sotto voce* under the continuing barrage of questions. 'And no air conditioning or closed doors, thank God.'

'If it salves your conscience any,' my sister murmurs back, 'that lintel was neither bought nor yanked off. Presented-in-appreciation-of-charitable-services-rendered. She told me.'

Abruptly the barrage stops. 'What are you talking about? . . . Go and wash up, children. We've put you in what used to be the harem.'

Three rooms to the side of the house open out on to a courtyard completely enclosed by high stone walls, shaded by a mango tree at one end and a jackfruit at the other. 'And no doubt a eunuch standing guard in between,' my sister mutters. 'So much for the good old days.'

'What eunuch?' at once the old voice demands eagerly behind us. 'Where, where?'

7

Day after tomorrow, driving home from the airport, my sister will probably warn him: 'Listen, your bugging devices are nothing compared to our old lady, so just you watch out.' Sitting between them, I shall be able to look from one profile to the other, maybe against a wet darkness blurring past the windows, light rain falling. As a child, remember being most still when most happy, unable to move lest the brimming moment spill. 'It's all right,' he will say, unperturbed. 'I've got used to you scrutable Orientals by now.' But we forget: the old lady speaks no English, except for one word. Might otherwise leave him alone, aside from a constant unwinking scrutiny when he is in sight, meanwhile pelting us with questions, plying him with food and uttering her one English word. 'Eat,' she will say benevolently. 'Eat, eat . . .' 'Just like my mother,' he will groan. Even so she will not perpetually smile like her niece, our hostess, and make small talk, mouth flattening sweet and smug across pretty white teeth; nor, like our host, introduce him to officials: military officials, government officials, business officials – an avalanche of bureaucratic handshaking from which he may never recover.

Even to conjecture the scene, here on this first day of my visit, makes me quail. 'Sightseeing,' my sister whispers. 'That's the answer. We'll take him out sightseeing morning, noon and night until we leave.' By evening we have already become conspirators, truly contemporaries as we escape the house to pitch our moment's presence against the entrancing centuried town. Walking down the narrow bazaar lanes, we practise translating the names of things into English, all for his delectation when he should arrive day after tomorrow. ('Look, the green gourd in the basket. That's *dil pasand*, Heart's Choice. And that knobbly one over there – that's called *kala kand*, the Root of Art. It's true, I swear it!')

But how to translate the untranslateable: exactly what it means to hear these languages sounding together again, plosive to fricative like clapper to bell: liquid Hindi phrases decorating a vegetable; harsh clatter of Marathi haggling in a market; pure classical Urdu spoken by the old retainers at the tombs of the Muslim saints, and by the caretaker declaiming to us at the Chakki, an ancient flour mill with its creaking water-wheel still in use –

'The water comes in underground tunnels from an unknown source in the hills seven miles away,' the caretaker enunciates slowly and deeply and beautifully into pale gold evening light, as if he were reciting a poem. Day after tomorrow perhaps a question to be translated: How can it be unknown if you know it is seven miles away? Are you sure no one ever found it – neither engineer nor sanitary inspector, not even the urchins playing in the hills or a cowherd grazing his flock? Today we listen, my sister and I: belief is sustenance, like the water itself.

'Mian Mohur.' The name resounds majestically on the caretaker's tongue, his delivery rising in grandeur from ode to epic. 'Mian Mohur, the hunchback slave who became our Prime Minister in 1600. It was he who installed this water supply and we can still use it safely, all our townspeople, all these centuries later.'

It churns over the wheel, splashes down exquisitely carved and inlaid channels, past formal gardens (sunlight, grass, croton leaves) to a place of pure white minarets and petalled arches, fluted pillars and marble floors. 'Sshh, listen –' A mosque. Within, the chanting sounds and stops and sounds again. We move away, not to disturb.

'You know,' I tell her, 'this is one of the things I've most missed, being away from home.' How can I explain it? Only hands can gesture together, showing her everything coalesced – not just sunlight, grass, croton leaves, but a total opposite of what it was like abroad where I have lived since my marriage. 'Life was somehow so compartmentalized there. One language at a time. One era at a time. One religion at a time. Except for the cities, which were another problem entirely, everything else was pruned down to stay in its place, very tidy. No bursting of boundaries, of things spilling over into your life willynilly, like this jumble of languages and religions and the past and the present that we are smitten with here. Yes, that was perhaps the most cramping of all: the business of being caught perpetually and irretrievably within your own time-span; clutching the present, being clutched by the present. . . .'

'Inevitable, though, isn't it?' Thoughtfully my sister traces the outline of a leaf with her forefinger. 'After all, theirs is a different idiom of existence, so they are bound to possess a different sense of time. Don't you see? For us it is an underpinning, such a constant dimension that without it we are well and truly lost. Meaning, if the past can cripple us, it can also provide our crutches. For whatever that's worth.' Yes, we've both learned that, culturally as well as personally, our respective marriages having taken us toward the same insight from opposite ends – I in rebelling against tradition, she in accepting it. After a pause, she adds: 'Did you know that the language in some of the Vedic texts has no present tense? Because the moment a word is uttered, it is past.'

Typically, while I am still mulling over that, she has a practical prescription to offer. 'Tell you what, let's go to the caves tomorrow.'

'Marabar?' I laugh. No, not the mythical Marabar; just Buddhist caves here in the bare northern hills overlooking the town: dark, unpretentious, a little smudged by time.

'Carved between the 5th century B.C. and the 2nd century A.D,' our guide Abdulla waves a reckless hand the next day. What's a couple of centuries more or less? Our hosts have insisted he accompany us on the expedition (impossible to contemplate two young women going off unescorted to that lonely hillside), but we like the young rascal: the way he stood shock-headed, solemnly at attention while being interviewed in the big house; the way he now goes whistling, chattering, throwing out casual snippets of information – mostly inaccurate – as he picks his way over thorn and pebble and scrub to reach the easternmost cave.

Last time I was here, it was a friend who took us around: a meticulous, erudite man; dates and trends and theories holding their shape in his mind as palpably as the shapes of *chaitya* and *vihara* around us. This time we have no need of annotations – enough to know, outside, the feel of sunwarmed stone at fingertips; inside, the musty smell of bats and centuries; and from far away the sound of a child's voice floating faintly into the dimness. We turn to each other, struck by the same thought.

'Listen to that, Abdulla. More people coming up the hill. Why don't you go and show them around, that way you have two groups of clients at one trip? We can wait for you here.'

'Here' is a boulder perched on the hillside, slightly askew but with the huge and solid certainty of Krishna's butter-ball. Abdulla wavers, his feet turned towards the exit, his face half-turned towards us in doubt. 'Yesterday there were goondas here, such hooligans! Don't know where they came from. Luckily they didn't deface anything, but they threw stones at tourists and tried to dislodge rocks and hack at the roots of trees to bring them down. I don't know if I should –'

'Don't worry, it's all right. Really. Look, if we sit on this boulder we'll be within your view all the time, so you can keep an eye on us as you promised.' She smiles reassuringly at him; succumbing, he grins back – a broad delighted gleam of teeth in the darkness – and disappears.

'Devious, aren't you?'

'Certainly.' Unabashed, she scrambles up after me. Not since our teens have we felt such a gleeful sense of playing truant, flouting censure ('Graceless, two grown women climbing rocks like monkeys!'), sitting there with our saris billowing around us. It was she who draped a sari on me, when I first wore it to school, admonishing sternly: No pins. No long strides.

'Remember that?'

We don't talk together so much as simply be together, using not sentences so much as spaces shared – for those we both love; for filling in blanks; for pooling the discoveries of our separate lives (how in my foreign flat privacy can change to loneliness, how in her bustling joint-family home companionship can turn to chaos); catapulting back and forth from the past to the possible; ranging at random over books read, pictures seen, people met, clothes worn; moving from experience to insight; from language to dialect to the kinship of silence.

Especially here, the reason for our pilgrimage. 'It's not only the stone, even the stillness here is sculptured. Have you noticed?'

I notice: Abdulla's whistle can't penetrate it, nor the chattering family he escorts. (Father sporting dark glasses, mother a wad of betel leaf in her cheek; twin sons with breaking voices and downy upperlips; a small girl in a vivid red skirt.) Silence is what the Buddhist monks have left behind in this place, carved as carefully as their caves: the accumulated peace of their years of discipline and meditation. Met with thrice before, recognized again, this quiet that is not disturbed by noise – once in a Thai temple; once in a synagogue in Cochin; once, unforgettably, in that mountain village in Japan, tucked away behind the hills, so remote you could fool yourself into believing fate couldn't touch you there.

Shrilly the family troops out of one cave and into another. Teeth gleaming, Abdulla follows. Above us the sky turns hazy with heat; a kite circles, lazily watchful. In front, the hill falls away in a series of bumpy slopes to the plateau below: at one end of it, a potter's village (narrow streets, women carrying brass pitchers balanced on their heads) and at the other, almost directly beneath us, the ruined splendour of the Empress's Golden Palace, very 17th-century Moghul, gaudy and sombre at once.

On cold nights the wind must whistle eerily through those broken arches; today it blends faint noises from the town. Small deliberate creak of the Chakki's water wheel, clang of cycle bells, human hum of the bazaar, mechanical sounds from a crew of men laying a new road just around the bend of the hill and out of sight: a dull banging, whirring, drilling, pause; banging, whirring, drilling, pause, – suddenly a deafening explosion.

Everything moves. Dizzy, I turn to my sister, find her staring back at me equally startled, one rueful eyebrow climbing her forehead. 'Don't tell me I'm pregnant again.'

'You couldn't be. I felt it too.'

'Oh, it's the dynamite, silly. From the road.'

She has scarcely finished speaking when there is another explosion, louder than the first. With it, a rumbling, a sliding. Our rock pitches forward and we are thrown off balance, scrabbling frantically at its surface for a handhold. 'Let's get out of here.' But we can't. Try to move, and the boulder teeters again, rolling forward another few inches before coming precariously to rest just short of a small rocky ledge.

'Don't move!' Abdulla has come running out; his terrified face sets the seal on our danger.

Then this must be one of the rocks that the hooligans tried to dislodge yesterday for the pleasure of seeing it hurtle downhill. What they began anything can complete at any moment – another reverberation, our slightest movement, a sneeze. The ledge might break our fall; it might not. The entire family surrounds Abdulla now, circle of frozen upturned faces staring at us, we staring back, petrified until made part of the boulder in a desperate travesty of stillness. – My heart thudding or hers? So loud, so violent, it might shake the boulder, send us crashing down, ending . . .

'Buttress it –' Again caught by the same thought, we can scarcely whisper. Somehow the father understands and forestalls us, suddenly galvanized into authority. 'Stones. Pick up the heaviest you can find and lay them against the base of the boulder. We can try to keep it from moving. You, Amol –' A quick stream of Bengali to one of the twins and the boy takes off, running zigzag down the steps of the hill followed by his mother's anxious cry. Perhaps 'Be careful, you might fall!' Again the father interrupts, brusque. 'Sshh, no noise. Come on, Abdulla. Hurry.'

Time topples . . . slowed down to their every movement: a nightmare choreography, their bending down, picking up each stone, staggering over with it, carefully lowering and easing it into place against our rock. May not work. Against the whole height of the hill, one small boy, now a dwindling brown streak still zigzagging down the bottom steps. Things happen in threes. Two blasts already. One more, and the end. No one speaks. The child says shrilly 'Ma? –' on a high note of fear. With a hand on her shoulder the mother turns her away, glancing briefly back at us, implacable, one-mother-to-another: *If anything should happen to you, I want to spare her the sight.*

Notice it all. Take in every detail to keep from shaking. Three dried grasses waving on the ledge. Black and ochre dust. My sister's blue sari on the rock, rock the colour of a water buffalo's back. Child's red skirt vanishing around a tree trunk. Remember the mother's look to recognize it afterwards if there is an afterwards. Now, childless, I must let my sister accept that look: having children she has more value. We are not only ourselves but what others have invested in us. – One more day. Please let me have one more day until he arrives tomorrow. Vertigo; falling; down into terror; no tomorrow. But cling. Cling to the thought of it; *until he comes tomorrow. Please.* Flesh has never been so sweet, to look, to touch, to be with one another, laugh over the names of vegetables – oh God, if prayer is so easy it couldn't be prayer.

As the fourth stone settles into place there is a slight bump, the rock begins to teeter. Watching Abdulla jump out of the way, we daren't move, breathe, clutch each other; but nothing happens. One more stone may do it, hold back the rock. If there isn't another blast, if the twin reaches in time to warn the road crew. Time. Not layers or tenses now but life itself. Runnels of sweat down back, down legs. Palms clammy; thighs damp against the rock. No need to ask what she is thinking. Never so close, never so separate; separate investments. Like joined twins being relentlessly torn apart, morsel by morsel of flesh and memory. Always complaining you didn't look alike in life, now perhaps in death you will, no more complaints, equally mangled – Stop it.

From the road a confused noise but no report. Amnesty once more. With it, a sudden ineradicable rage. Why, why, if this is to be the end, were these last vouchsafed days frittered away in hypocrisy, mouthing politenesses to our host and hostess; why not my husband here; her family; our parents – our lives are those we love.

JUMP. Have I said it aloud? Turn to her at last, unable to focus or see her face; only the eyes, familiar, loved, hazel-flecked; my older sister, my touchstone self commanding NO. SIT STILL. BE STILL. BE, become . . . Not dynamite exploding but all my

13

separate selves, from the centre outwards, from him, from what we have built between us, to become beggar's hunger, profiteer's greed, old woman's curiosity, embrace them each and die, stop the waiting; not half in love with easeful death but totally, totally, cool caved dark – Tomorrow. Think. Concentrate. Tomorrow. Without him, death may be impossible as life. *Tomorrow*.

If no explosion yet, probably never. The twin has reached. 'They're coming!' Shrill, it's the child again, resilient, red skirt bobbing up and down. She has come all the way from fear to excitement: A spectacle! Men with ropes, pulleys, axes on their shoulders; climbing slowly, tortuously up the jagged steps. In abeyance now, the chaos, the anger, the unbearable love – And for her? Next to me, a still, beautiful blur, what is she thinking, what am I thinking, going off at tangents, always talking to him in my head: 'Stupid, isn't it, having to stave off terror by watching yourself stave off terror?'

With help on the way we can force ourselves to look down now, concede the worst: rock, hillside, gravity, pulling you down into death. Infinitesimal too, our deaths like our lives, mere scratches on Mian Mohur's water system, just two more dead for the Golden Palace. Now, saved from it, it is possible to entertain the idea, entertaining idea, death.

Pulleys; men; noise. Ropes flung tight around the belly of our rock and fastened to a tree trunk at either end. Barricade of stones built higher. Brown, sinewy arms streaked with sweat; hot heavy breathing in the sun; palms flattened, braced against the boulder. Peremptory order: 'Now jump.'

We jump. Saris billow behind; absurd parachutes. Alive, alive. Safe. At least for the moment. Tell them, thank them. Mouth dry, hand at last clutching her, as if never to let go. 'You saved our lives –' Invitations to dinner; baksheesh; gratitude; recompense absurd as parachutes, all the way down the steps of the hill to the potters' village below (through narrow dusty streets, past women balancing pitchers on their heads); pebbles underfoot; reek of drains and cowdung; to where our hosts' car awaits, handing time back to us – stolid anachronism, parked next to the Golden Palace.

Stepping in, I hear her pause and turn to Abdulla. All this time, noticing and noticing, I haven't noticed his face: waxen, still terrified, skin pulled perilously taut across high cheekbones. 'Of course it wasn't your fault,' she is saying crisply. 'After all, we suggested it ourselves. Didn't we? How on earth were *you* supposed to know the boulder was pried loose? I'll tell them that. Don't worry. We'll sign a paper, if you like.'

As a guide, his reputation would have died with us. Still very well might. But suddenly, nerves frayed endlessly beneath the endlessly burning sun, I turn on her in exasperation, protesting in our dialect – blessed obscure dialect that nobody here understands – 'Will you stop being so impossibly good? You're too much, worrying about him after what we've been through.'

She glares at me, annoyed in return, not saintly in the least. 'Damn it, it's his livelihood, isn't it? We are safe now, it's all over. What about *him*?' Again that parental heritage: no vehement claims on virtue, merely this willingness to take each moment wholly and then leave it as wholly behind: receive and relinquish with open hands. Theirs after all is the same wisdom that sang the Vedas in the past tense.

She has always possessed that. It is I who need to go on innumerable journeys, almost die, to learn; meanwhile slowly counting my age by birthdays of knowledge.

Above us the caves are pitted dark and high in the hillside; here the broken archways of the Golden Palace wear the sky proudly, like an immense blue crown.

The Schoolmaster

Our village is especially proud of three things – the temple, the local idiot, and the Middle School.

We are proud of the temple because, for one thing, it is the earliest example of Pallava architecture in India, and learned men are always coming down from Madras University to exclaim over the grace and balance of its sculpture. For another – and this is far more important to us – there is a splendid old pipal tree beside it, its branches hung with fluttering pieces of white cloth tied there by pilgrims as votive offerings in return for prayers granted. It is a pretty reliable tree on the whole; at any rate, the pilgrims have been increasing every year, and with them the temple revenue.

The local idiot is something of a mascot. Old Mother (we call her that as a sign of our respect and affection), who lives down at the corner of the street, tells of the night he was born – of a wandering sadhu who visited the village and pronounced a special blessing, declaring that hereafter the child was under his spiritual protection. Its mother lived just long enough to hear the blessing, and managed to smile, but the sadhu turned to Old Mother and said under his breath, 'The child needs it. Look after him,' after which he walked out of the door into the darkness and was never seen again. So the idiot went into Old Mother's care – a huge, witless boy who roamed the streets uttering raucous, discordant noises and slavering with excitement every time he saw a bicycle or a car. Once when Old Mother went to the city to visit relatives, she brought back a tin of polish and gave it to him. After that, he made a living polishing bicycles or an occasional motorcar. A legend had grown up that the sadhu's blessing affected not only the idiot but his surroundings as well – as long as he lived in our village it would be safe from disaster; his presence insured our luck.

Whether from coincidence or otherwise, it was true that catastrophes that struck the surrounding areas passed lightly by our

17

village. During days of famine, the temple granaries were full enough to prevent any deaths from starvation. When drought ravaged the south, we had sufficient water from a new well dug near Old Mother's house, on a spot designated by one of the pilgrims, who happened to be a water diviner. It was the exact place where the idiot usually sat on a stump making earsplitting noises with a plantain-leaf whistle, and this, it was concluded, was further evidence of the sadhu's blessing, and revealed the inarticulate wisdom of the idiot himself. Hadn't he chosen the place every day, and hadn't we been fools enough not to recognize his message?

It was the idiot again who gave the zamindar's car its extra-shiny coat of polish. Evoking, we were positive, not only praise for his efforts but a most unexpected and generous donation to the village Middle School – an endowment in memory of a favourite son, who had died young. With the new capital, we would be able to hire teachers at our own discretion instead of being dependent upon the government. This made our school the only one of its kind within a radius of fifty miles. And somehow it became a point of honour with all the villagers to contribute what they could to run it. Children were sent regularly, and Old Mother took it upon herself to deliver a stinging lash of her tongue to any indifferent parents who preferred to have their offspring help in the fields rather than sit in school all day.

Old Mother was, in fact, so interested in the working of the school that when the old master was transferred to a government school and the school board held a meeting to decide about a new master, she insisted on being allowed to attend the meeting, or at least have a verbatim report of it from the village headman, or *karnam*. Our *karnam* has always been a mild-mannered man, and even years of being headman have not altered his innate courtesy. He sat patiently in her little two-room house and told her what had happened.

The school board had advertised for a teacher in the national papers, and received five letters of application. Two had been dismissed at once because the writers were so absurdly young. 'Barely twenty-one, would you believe it?' said the *karnam*, and Old Mother shook her head in bewilderment at the new ways. The third letter had been arrogantly worded; the applicant had wanted to know whether there were any cinema theatres in the village, and how many miles we were from the nearest city. As it happened, there *was* a theatre newly opened in the village, but Old Mother agreed with the *karnam* that this preoccupation with cinemas did not seem the right attitude for a man who would be in charge of moulding the minds of young children. 'The fourth was out of the question,' the *karnam* said emphatically. 'Too many degrees. We know that kind.' Old Mother nodded again. She believed firmly that a head could be crammed with just so much; beyond that, the balance would be upset.

They arrived at the fifth applicant, Mr Sharma. The drawback here was that Mr Sharma was from the north, and a stranger to our ways. But his letter, expressing all that he wanted to do in his work with children, had touched the *karnam*, though Mr Patel, the owner of the theatre, had warned that too much theory detracted from the practice of anything – from teaching children to tapping toddy. However, this was Mr Patel's hobbyhorse, so the board had chosen to ignore the warning and had hired the man. 'Besides,' the *karnam* said proudly, remembering the new school funds, 'we can always sack him if he is not suitable, and get someone else.'

Almost the whole village waited beneath the banyan tree when Mr Sharma's horse-drawn jutka came clattering down the dusty road from the railway station ten miles away. He was a small, thin man, rather nondescript, with spectacles and an unexpectedly charming one-sided smile. His clothes were white and hand-spun, which met with our approval, for after Gandhiji came to our village, two years before he died, we had started a cooperative handloom shop, and every man, woman and child in the village knew how to spin. And through the open neck of his shirt Old Mother glimpsed the sacred thread, which was equally satisfactory, for it showed he was a Brahman and could be expected to know the classical texts.

The *karnam* welcomed Mr Sharma. Mr Sharma smiled back his thanks, and his eyes sought the children, who stood clustered to one side, watching him suspiciously.

They were still suspicious when they dragged their feet, half-unwilling, half-fascinated, to school next morning.

We grown-ups waited at home, wondering how things were going. At lunchtime, there was a collective joyous yell from the school, and the children rushed out chattering and throwing their schoolbags into the air. The schoolmaster was a success.

Such an immediate success that Mr Patel took to muttering 'Just you wait and see . . .' We waited, but nothing happened. The children loved their school now. They had some classes in the mango grove, which roused the disapproval of the elders in the village; they put on plays and dramatized stories from the ancient Puranas, which mollified those who had disapproved; they had a natural-history club and went on rambles across the countryside, watching birds and collecting tadpoles; they even had a camera, which Mr Sharma bought them with his own money, and learned how to develop film. For almost two months, the village was too astounded to make much comment. The third month, we slowly got used to Mr Sharma's unorthodox ways. For in spite of the love of tradition implicit in his dramatization of the Puranas, he had taught the children to be unafraid and ask questions. He himself was unafraid, and even told the school board off over some crisis in the ordering of textbooks. We heard of this with bated breath, and spoke of it in whispers. Then came the incident with the zamindar's weekend guests.

Our zamindar is far from the kind of zamindar they are always portraying in films from Madras and Bombay – bloated on the fat of the land, seducing innocent village maidens when they are drawing water from the well. He is an absent-minded old soul who spends most of his time looking up and down the country for the right guru. About once every three years, he thinks he has found his ideal spiritual mentor; then something about the saint disappoints him and he begins the quest all over again. Our village had seen one child saint from the south, one woman saint from the north, and about six holy men gathered separately from different areas. They were brought in turn to live in the zamindar's house, down by the river to the south of the village, until each went out of favour and was sent back to wherever he or she had come from.

This house is hidden from view by a mango grove, and hesitates on the brink of a splendid stretch of rice fields. The fields are barely a fraction of what the zamindar's estate once was, before the government passed the Zamindari Abolition Bill. Then he was counted a minor rajah, and he and his family, as chief landlords of the district, owned not only the land in and around our village but two of the neighbouring villages as well. Today he retains the title and much of the prestige, but his present property is confined to the Home Fields – those cultivated under his personal supervision – and the enormous white house by the river, which he and his son use, respectively, for devotional meetings and weekend parties. In compensation for the land that was given to his tenants, the

20

government pays the zamindar a substantial sum every year, and it is said that much of it has gone to meet the expenses of this son, who stayed abroad many years and then returned home, greatly addicted to parties.

On whichever weekend the son decided to entertain, cars would drive in from the city, their brilliant headlights swinging around the curve by the banyan tree, past the theatre and the well and the wayside stalls, and then turning left down the bumpy road that leads to the mango grove and the house beyond. Beginning with a flash of chromium and ending with a cloud of dust, they were plangent intrusions from a different world, honking their way impatiently through our narrow village streets. Startled housewives dropped their pots, and babies sleeping by the windows began to wake and scream. Some of us muttered a little, but the *karnam* promptly squelched any impertinence; agricultural reforms might come and go, but the zamindar was still the rajah of the neighbourhood. There was less complaint about the sounds of laughter and revelry that floated through the rice-scented darkness later in the night. The visitors might be in our village, but they were of another world, and, with a tolerance bred in our blood down the centuries, we left them alone.

Except for the children. The children squished across the rice fields and hung over the fence looking into the windows of the big house, sucking their fingers and staring wide-eyed at the people and lights and rich clothes until the caretaker found them there and shooed them off. Once, they spied some white-skinned foreigners – one of them with hair the colour of a ripe *badami* mango – and came scuttling back to the village to tell the tale. That night, a trail of villagers stepped single file through the fields and gazed at this marvel until the caretaker got after *them* as well, and shooed the whole crowd off.

The *karnam* decided to stop this ridiculous nonsense, as he called it. 'Why stare so?' he demanded indignantly of Old Mother. 'They're people, aren't they?'

Old Mother chewed her betel leaf and gave him a smile of great and toothless tolerance. 'So are we,' she said comfortably. 'So we're curious. *Ayyo*, let it be. So you scold them today, so the cityfolk leave tomorrow, so we all forget it the day after. Let it be.'

We continued to let it be. The parties had grown much quieter, and the schoolmaster explained, with a grin, that this was probably due to prohibition. He explained about prohibition, too, and why

21

the government had banned liquor throughout the state. The children listened dutifully, and translated it all in terms of Minu. Minu was a slender little creature, seven years old, who sat at the desk by the door and stared out sorrowfully, because her father was a toddy tapper and prohibition meant he was out of a job. Mr Sharma was helping him find another, but Minu continued to stare sorrowfully out of the door and the boys thought she was beautiful. So, to cheer her up, they took her with them on a midnight jaunt to the zamindar's house to view the latest lot of weekend guests.

This time, the party was noisier than usual. There was much clinking of glasses and pouring of liquid from bottles; there were guffaws, and screams, and other raucous noises of enjoyment. Soon it got so noisy that the villagers began to waken and stir, and Minu and her friends prudently decided to get back to bed before the grownups discovered their absence.

But their decision came a moment too late. Some of the guests had walked out into the garden, and a big red-faced man, catching sight of the cluster of children huddled over the fence, moved up noiselessly, thrust out a big hand, and caught hold of Minu's skirt and dragged her forward. '*Ah!*' he boomed. 'What pretty thing do we have here?'

Minu screamed, and the rest of the children jumped over the fence to her rescue, only to be forced back by a tight circle of strangers who completely surrounded the little girl, pinching her cheek and asking questions in loud voices. Minu blinked back her tears and stared at them with silent, concentrated fury, until the boys lowered their heads, butted their way through the circle in a whirl of lashing fists and kicks, and bore her off to safety over the fence.

This was when Mr Sharma entered the picture. Faced with the prospect of going home to a scolding from their parents, and with a trembling Minu on their hands, the children turned their steps towards the schoolhouse and knocked on the schoolmaster's door. A sleepy voice answered, footsteps shuffled across the room, the latch slid back, and Mr Sharma stood gazing down at the upturned faces. He rubbed his eyes and looked again. One of the boys, Mr Patel's nephew, gulped and began to explain. But Mr Sharma, with a lack of curiosity unheard of in grownups, stopped him with a gesture and motioned them into his room. There he heated milk for them to drink and sat holding Minu close until her shivering stopped, while he listened in silence to the story.

'They were so *big*.' Minu quavered suddenly, speaking for the first time. 'They were so big and tall, and they stood around me . . .'

Patel's nephew told us later that he had never seen the schoolmaster so angry. But when he spoke, his voice was quiet, as always. 'It's all right,' he said. 'I'll speak to the zamindar about it. But don't go there again when there is so much clinking of glasses.'

Next morning, before the story had time to get around, the schoolmaster closed his door behind him and walked purposefully across the fields to the mango grove and the house beyond. The caretaker saw him coming, took him to the dining room, where the zamindar's son was dawdling over his breakfast, and stood behind the door as a matter of course to listen to what was happening – which is how the village came to know about it.

'Yes?' the young zamindar enquired. 'What can I do for you?' So early in the morning, his manner implied. He gazed at the schoolmaster with puffy-eyed distaste across the breakfast table.

The schoolmaster recounted, in level tones, what had happened the night before.

'Well,' the young zamindar said when Mr Sharma had finished, 'what do you expect me to do about it?'

'I expect you to tell your guests to keep their hands off the village children,' the schoolmaster replied equably.

The young zamindar's temper and left eyebrow began to rise at the same time. 'Why the devil should I? It isn't as if they raped the kid –'

'No,' Mr Sharma agreed. 'They didn't. But by the time the story gets around the village, that is what it will have become.'

'What happens in the village is none of your business.'

'Minu is my business,' Mr Sharma said. 'I teach the children –'

'Then why the hell don't you teach them not to trespass on other people's property? They deserve what they get, the miserable little devils.'

'They were not trespassing,' the schoolmaster corrected quietly. 'They were outside the fence, and your friends pulled the child in.'

'They were staring over it, which is just as bad, if not worse. All that vulgar curiosity –'

'Wasn't it equally vulgar curiosity on the part of you and your friends to drag a child in against her will and frighten her with impossible questions?'

The young zamindar leaped to his feet. 'Of all the impertinence!' he shouted. 'I will not have you insulting my friends under my roof. Get out!'

Mr Sharma stood up, too. 'All right,' he said, 'I'll get out. But first I must tell you this. If any of your friends ever dare touch a village child again, I shall report you to the police for having illicit liquor in the house.'

The young man stared. 'Are you *blackmailing* me?' he asked at last.

'Not really,' Mr Sharma said. 'Not if you leave the children alone.'

In the silence that followed, the old zamindar entered the room, clearing his throat in embarrassed little spurts.

The caretaker told us that the atmosphere changed after this. The old zamindar asked a good many vague questions and sat knitting his eyebrows, trying to sort out the replies. Finally, his son walked out of the room in exasperation, and the old man leaned across the table and offered Mr Sharma a cup of coffee. 'Forgive an old man's curiosity,' he said, 'and tell me, what made you think up this – ummm – this blackmailing stunt?'

For the first time that morning, Mr Sharma laughed. 'I lost my head,' he admitted. 'But I kept remembering Minu's eyes –'

'Minu?' the old man asked.

'Her father is a toddy tapper,' Mr Sharma said. 'The man loses his job because of prohibition, while your son's bootlegging friends get drunk on cocktails and torment his daughter. How's that for fairness?'

The zamindar sighed. 'Yes,' he said. 'It is hard.'

'Hard nothing,' Mr Sharma said, vigorously stirring the sugar in his coffee. 'Don't you see, all *our* conflicts are finding expression in that unfortunate child. God knows how many worlds are destined to meet in her, poor thing.'

'D'you mean she might marry a foreigner?' the old zamindar said brightly.

Mr Sharma drank down his coffee very fast. 'I have to go,' he said. 'Thank you very much for your kindness.'

But the old man's attention had strayed. 'Tell me again,' he said. 'How do you think my son looks?'

The schoolmaster paused a moment, and then his honesty got the better of him. 'He looks like a dissipated child of forty,' he said, and

24

waited for the storm to break.

But, to his amazement, the old zamindar nodded. 'He isn't forty yet,' he said. 'I worry about my son.' Then he looked up at the schoolmaster and his eyes shone. 'You have insight into the hearts of men,' he said. 'You recognize the quality of each one's spirit. Minu's. My son's. Mine. Tell me – have you ever considered becoming a guru?'

At this, Mr Sharma took fright. He stammered his denials and his thanks all at the same time, and fled down the drive before the zamindar could utter another word. By the time he reached the sanctuary of his room and got ready for classes, opinions in the village were already clashing over his unsuspecting head.

The caretaker, as our chief informant, was pro-Sharma by inclination but pro-zamindar by loyalty – after all, he reminded us, he'd served the zamindars all his life. Mr Patel's two older nephews, home after the benefit of a university education in the city, found in the schoolmaster a champion of democracy and fundamental rights. Old Mother chewed her betel leaf and said, 'Well, I don't know about all that, but he certainly knows the classical texts.' And the *karnam* and his entire faction believed that the schoolmaster had gone too far. It was shameless, it was brazen effrontery, it was impudence of the worst kind, adopting that tone to the zamindar. No one in the village had ever done it. *No* one.

'Feudalism,' said the Patel nephews.

'Courtesy,' said the *karnam*. 'Respect.'

Meanwhile, the caretaker was nagged by a mysterious detail he couldn't fathom. Mr Sharma had mentioned a chicken drink, he remembered – a drink made from a part of a chicken – that had intoxicated the weekend guests. And we all put our heads together and tried to discover what this could be, until it eventually dawned on the Patel brothers. They roared and slapped each other on the back and roared again, and then explained it to the rest of us – which is how our village was first introduced to the cocktail.

Through all this, the schoolmaster continued to teach and talk to the children, and to show Minu all of his books and pictures and gentleness until the distress of her memory slowly blurred. But he refused to see any of the adults; he even, politely and firmly, refused to discuss the affair with the *karnam*. We can only guess how it would finally have ended if the idiot hadn't taken it into his head to shower his patronage on the schoolmaster. He followed him

25

to classes and sat crooning with delight in the last row; followed him to his room and sat swatting flies by the door. He polished the schoolmaster's dilapidated old bicycle about six times a day, until it collapsed beneath so much attention. And Mr Sharma took it all quietly and without comment. To the village, the idiot's favour, recalling as it did the sadhu's blessing, seemed to vindicate the schoolmaster. The dissenting voices gradually subsided, and he was reinstated to his position and again treated with the dignity accorded a scholar.

At this point, perhaps all that Mr Sharma wanted was to be left alone, but the old zamindar hadn't forgotten him and was determined to thrust whatever greatness he could upon the schoolmaster. He increased the grant to the school, making provision for raising Mr Sharma's salary, and even bought a little house around the corner from the school, furnished it, and had the school board allocate it for the schoolmaster's use.

When the *karnam* came round to the schoolmaster's room one night with the information about the house, Mr Sharma's jaw dropped. 'For God's sake,' he begged. 'Tell him thanks, and tell him to leave me alone.' Which was iconoclasm all over again, and the *karnam* was opening his mouth to administer a sharp rebuke when the idiot made a small crooning noise at the door. The *karnam* remembered the holy man's blessing, and held his peace.

So the schoolmaster moved to the little house and walked to school every morning as the sun climbed over the top of the banyan tree, and walked back again after classes as the temple bell rang for evening worship. We were beginning to take him for granted as part of the village landscape.

Then, as abruptly as he had taken up the schoolmaster, the idiot transferred his affections elsewhere – back to the plantain-leaf whistle and a field on the other side of the village, where he sat throwing stones at birds and making his earsplitting noises. And the Patel brothers moved north, where they had found jobs. Without ever being quite aware that he had them, the schoolmaster lost his three most ardent supporters. Shortly after this, the zamindar and his son went abroad for the summer, and the house by the river was closed and empty. So when the rumour about the schoolmaster began, there was nobody to refute it with enough conviction or authority – except, perhaps, Old Mother. 'Talks to himself when he goes home from school?' she repeated incredulously. 'I don't believe a word of it. He's probably reciting the classical texts.'

26

'No,' the *karnam* said grimly. 'That he doesn't, let me assure you. No one who recites the classical texts would behave as he did with the zamindar –'

'Sometimes you're more half-witted than my idiot,' Old Mother declared. 'Why rake up that old rubbish now, you foolish man? And why on earth shouldn't he talk to himself if he wants to? I talk to myself, too,' she added proudly.

'Not the way this man talks,' the *karnam* said. 'Carrying on long conversations . . .' He drooped his underlip, and then he tapped his temple with his index finger and shrugged.

'No,' Old Mother insisted. 'There must be a reason.'

Minu could have told them that reason. She had stopped Mr Sharma one day and asked, 'Teacher, why do you talk to yourself?' And the schoolmaster replied, 'For the simple reason, Minu, that there is no one else in your village to whom I *can* talk. I find myself a perfect listener.'

But the village thought otherwise. And the rumour grew and grew. And Mr Patel, looking important, found the ideal opportunity to say, 'I told you so.'

'What I can't understand,' Old Mother protested, 'is why nobody noticed it before this.'

'Ah,' said Mr Patel, 'that's because he didn't have a home to walk back to, talking to himself. Nobody saw him talking when he was living in the schoolhouse. Now we can see him and we *know*. Though I said all along that too much theory detracts from the practice. . . . In any case, what can you practise when you have lost your reason? It is dangerous leaving little children in a madman's charge.'

'Yes,' said the *karnam*, and 'yes,' said the village, it was dangerous leaving the children in his charge. And everybody except the children thought it wisest to sack Mr Sharma and hire another teacher with the newly augmented school funds.

The *karnam* went to relay our decision to the schoolmaster, and, as we had on his first day with us, again we waited at home, wondering what the outcome would be. Whatever reaction we expected, it was certainly not this: Mr Sharma grinned. 'Yes,' he said. 'I expected that, and I'm glad.'

'What do you mean?' the *karnam* demanded, indignant. 'Aren't you sorry to leave?'

'To leave the children, yes,' said Mr Sharma, tempering truth with his charming one-sided smile. 'Otherwise, I don't think so. I'm

27

afraid all this worship was making me rather uncomfortable.'

'Worship?'

'Yes, worship. You worship the zamindar, and the zamindar worships me. I'll be glad to get away before he comes back and turns me into a guru.'

For a moment, the *karnam* was too outraged to speak. At last, he managed to sputter, 'Will you please leave this village –'

'– as soon as possible,' Mr Sharma concluded obligingly. 'Of course I will.' And he packed his bags.

Next morning, we gathered in rather a shamefaced group beneath the banyan tree to see the schoolmaster off. Old Mother had cooked crisp sweet rice balls for him and packed them in a little brass container, which she piled with the rest of his luggage. The children crowded around him, some of them crying, all of them bearing farewell gifts, and he turned and smiled at them before he climbed in. They ran in a little straggling group to keep pace with the jutka, following it as far as they could and then dropping out one by one as the clip-clop of the horse's hoofs died away in the distance and all that was left of Mr Sharma was the dust raised by the jutka wheels.

Minu refused to eat for about a week afterwards, and moped for another month. But it took our village much longer to realize what we had done. The summer had to pass; a succession of schoolmasters had to come, be found wanting, and go; the zamindar had to return and bewail the loss of an incipient guru before we came to our senses. Of course, there was no trace to be found of the man. So we did just what he would never have wanted: we worshipped him in retrospect.

Now our village is especially proud of four things – the temple, the local idiot, the Middle School, and the schoolmaster who lived with us for a few memorable months and then left, because we were too ignorant to make him a guru and he was too wise to become one.

Letter . . .

And here in this Himalayan village, my dear one, the days are full of peace; sunlight has mellowed the harvest sheaves in the valley below, and at night the wooden houses are warm against the mountain wind.

I can see them from my window, their crooked brown roofs crowded together in haphazard, higgledy-piggledy fashion on either side of the white road. The road winds from the hillside down to the valley between the wooden houses until it reaches the fields and then stops, slightly astonished, before it goes bumping along over stubble and stone and disappears into the hills beyond.

The schoolchildren come running up this road every morning waving the cloth bags containing their slate and primary reader; their voices are shrill in the morning cold and their steps are light. Later there are herds of Himalayan goats with bells tinkling at their necks, snow-white and furry and plump, like little fat ladies. And still later there may be a caravan of mules from Tibet, coming up in a long and leisurely line, swishing their tails and waiting patiently outside the village shop until they are loaded with bags of salt, and then turning and winding their way slowly back towards Tibet again.

There is always a faint smell of resin in the village; of pinewood smoke curling lazily from twisted little chimneys or rising from the flare of pine-torches after dark. And always, too, there is the sound of bells: the tinkle as the goats go past, the sudden discordant clang from the village school, the deeptoned ringing from a Buddhist monastery on a nearby hill; and then a language of bells subtler yet and more delicate, as the women of the village walk down to the fields and the sound of their anklets is barely a whisper beneath their swaying skirts, blending with the soft cadences of their speech and echoing the rhythm of their life in the village. . . .

I watch them from my window and exclaim: 'I wish I could walk like that!'

'No,' says old Narayan very firmly. 'You cannot live like that, so you cannot walk like that. You may love the earth but your feet hardly touch it.'

And he picks up the old bronze lamp and takes it away to be cleaned while I gaze after him, completely taken aback. Narayan's flashes of insight amaze me more and more every day. You may not consider them particularly remarkable but then you, my dear one, do not know Narayan.

He has been in our family since my father was a boy, watching him grow to manhood and marry, and pronouncing a wholly satisfactory verdict of approval on my mother as a bride. Now, after all these years, he still recognizes her sweetness as much as he respects her strength; he knows too the worth of his own loyalty and devotion to them. Which is why, I suppose, he decided that his responsibility to the family was doubled when we were born. He spoilt us when we were babies and scolded us when we were children into eating the right food and going to bed at the right time and behaving like 'worthy children of noble parents' as he put it. And now that we are grown and will not be bossed, he considers it his self-imposed duty to lecture us on all possible occasions and remove any remaining nonsense from our heads. But none of us questions his authority: he has always been as sheltering as the roof above our heads – and just about as implacable.

Suddenly my heart warms to the old man in a renewed rush of gratitude. 'Narayan,' I call out to him. 'I thank you.'

He goes on cleaning the lamp – I can hear the scrapy sound of ashes on bronze – and only utters a noncommittal grunt.

'I mean it,' I persist. 'I thank you not only for all that you have done for us but also for escorting me to this place. If it hadn't been for you I could never have come here at all.' There is another grunt and I abandon the effort.

This new taciturnity is also a part of Narayan's new insight – or perhaps it was there all the time, only I never saw it because of our constant battles. He has always cherished my sister because she is beautiful in every way; he has adored my brother (though he would rather die than admit the fact) for carrying on the family 'name' and the family 'honour'; but towards me his attitude has ranged from mild disapproval to outright conflict and never did I imagine that he of all people would prove my staunchest ally in this last escapade of mine.

30

How can I tell you, my dear one, of the strangeness of my request to those I love most: that I who have returned to my country after three years and may be a bride within three months, should want to leave them all and go away to live alone in the mountains for a whole month? If it were a hill-station I wanted to visit, with friends-of-the-family sprinkled all over the neighbourhood or the usual available accommodation in an hotel, mine would not have been an unreasonable request.

But Nekhra is sixty miles from the nearest hill-station and has no telephone communication with the outside world. It is accessible only by a very narrow, very unpredictable mountain road that disappears off the face of the earth every time there is a snow-storm; there is just one rattling, antediluvian bus that comes – and more often does *not* come – every fortnight, bringing mail and a stray passenger or two to the village.

For a girl to live here alone and unescorted is absolutely unthinkable . . . and I hated to ask, as much as my parents hated to refuse. We had clearly reached an impasse when Narayan suddenly announced: 'I will go with her. I will see that she eats the right food and goes to bed at the right time.' After a second of generally dumbfounded silence my brother was heard to agree: 'She would *like* that, I'm sure!' But Narayan had already embarked upon one of his homilies. 'Everyone knows what the ancient texts have sanctioned,' he declared, 'about the stages in the life of a man. Your childhood, and then when you are a bachelor or a *brahmachari*; then *grahasth* with responsibilities to a household and family; and then the state of *vanaprasth* when your life's duties are ended and you retire to the forest to meditate – to evaluate your existence so that you may go to meet your death with a fuller understanding of life. . . . So if she wants her *vanaprasth* now,' he interrupted himself brusquely, 'let her have it'. My parents considered the idea; my brother murmured that you could always depend upon Narayan to equate everything to the sanction of the sacred texts; my sister chuckled and protested. 'But she isn't a man, is she, Narayan?' At which Narayan created another minor sensation by handing me the acme of all his compliments and ignoring my predictably furious reaction. 'No, but with her brains she should have been. It is hard to have the mind of a man and the heart of a woman. But do not worry, I shall look after her well –'

'– and lecture to her if she gets intractable,' concluded my brother with an irreverent grin, 'and tell her often and at length, what the sacred texts have decreed. . . .'

But strangely enough, Narayan neither lectures to me nor once mentions the sacred texts; he leaves me alone to come to terms with my soul and is generally uncommunicative – startling me only now and then, as with his awareness that the rhythm of my life is different from that of the women of Nekhra.

As different, my dear one, as is the rhythm of my country from the rhythm of yours. This I always knew, but here in this village I am beginning to understand it more deeply than ever before. And suddenly it frightens me. Suddenly and desperately I need to *talk* to someone, to say: 'I have to choose, and live with my decision – help me.' It is foolish . . . but I remember there is a cave on top of this hillside where it is said that holy men sometimes sit and meditate. I decide to go up there; and if there is one whom I can summon out of his wisdom and silence, I shall say: 'I feel I belong to neither world, tell me what I should do.'

Yes, it is foolish; it is against all my fine ideas of a lonely and independent decision. But what I want more than anything else now is advice from a stranger endowed with impersonal wisdom; so I rapidly snatch my black shawl and flinging it around my shoulders, rush out before I have time to change my mind.

Outside the air is crisp with a tang and a promise of cold in it. My little house, standing comfortably askew on the hillside, is soon left behind. In my unreasoning panic I slip on the grassy slopes and clutch for support at the trunks of the walnut trees. But with the scent of grass in the sunshine and the breeze light on my cheeks, I soon slacken my pace and pause to look around and know the beginning of a slow peace.

The nearer hills across the valley are shrouded in mist but the snow peaks rise above them, disembodied and dazzling white. Looking down, I can see the valley with the village held in its palm like a toy; and there above me, half-hidden beneath a mountain shrub and carved into a crag in the hillside, is the cave: cool and dark and . . . empty. There is not even one holy man – silent and ash-besmeared – to be seen anywhere.

I turn around in sudden blinding disappointment and stand still for a moment, unable to move, when there is a slight rustle in the bushes above me and a voice says quaintly in the hill-dialect: 'My greetings to you, lady-from-far-away!'

It is a child of about seven or eight, standing balanced on the edge of the crag, with the wind blowing her once-white clothes against her slender little body.

'And mine to you,' I manage to call back, smiling, after the first shock of finding that I am not alone after all. She laughs – a clear, tumbling sound in the sunlight – and clambers down the rock to join me. And that is how I meet Tara.

She is tiny, small-boned and delicate for this region of sturdy hill women; her grubby little hands are delicate too and the pure, pointed oval of her face has eyes that are enourmous and long lashed for a Mongolian race. 'Where are you from?' I ask her.

She waves her hand casually towards the snows of the north-east. 'Beyond *Choor Chandni*.'

'Choor Chandni?' – Fragments of the Moon: fragments as delicate as dust. . . .

'Yes, that one over there.' I follow her pointing finger to one peak, soaring alone into the sky, perfect in its purity and even more dazzling white than the rest. 'Don't you know that the girls of the village pray to it to bless their marriage?'

'No. Tell me.'

'On the night of the brightest moon in the month of *kartik* they light lamps and offer special prayers, and if Choor Chandni blesses them they will dream of the man they are to marry.' She elevates her small nose. 'But we don't do that, my sister and I: we don't belong to the village.'

'What are you doing here then?'

'My sister is sick. We have to wait until she recovers.' Her people, I discover, are nomads travelling to the nearest hill-station. 'It takes three days,' says Tara, matter-of-factly. 'We walk during the day and stop at night in the forest and light fires to keep the wild animals away.' She looks around her for a long stem of grass, snaps one off and starts to chew it. 'Where are *you* from?'

'From far away,' I smile at her, 'as you said in the beginning. How did you guess that?'

'Your clothes,' says Tara briefly. 'May I feel them?' Surprised and amused at her politeness, I nod and she fingers the delicate material of my sari with a quick, deft curiosity I am to discover increasingly in her. 'It's different. Is your home different too?'

And when I tell her that it is on the plains where the ground is flat and there are no hills and no valleys, she stands wide-eyed trying to imagine life without mountains and failing completely. Tara has lived in these mountains all her life. When they stop at a village like Nekhra that can boast of a school, she attends the classes; and when they resume their travels she takes her most prized possession with her – a tattered, dog-eared primary reader that she apparently knows by heart, for she recites it all from beginning to end in a high, sing-song chant as we walk down the hill together.

'– And *Guruji* says I am to be promoted and can go to a higher class and he will give me a new book and it won't be torn and I can study until my sister is well again and we have to leave.'

I look at her and am stirred to an ache of pity. A *tara* is a star and she does have a curiously star-like quality; a clear, rare sparkle that seems to acquire all the more depth in this remote mountain village. 'Who named you?' I ask her and she tells me it was the midwife from the hill-station who was called in when she was born.

'Because they thought we might die, my mother and I,' she adds by way of explanation, 'and the midwife's sister worked for a lady who was wise and good and beautiful and was called Tara.'

'You have a beautiful name,' I compliment her, 'and you know what it means. Live then your life well and like a *tara*.'

She accepts that gravely but says nothing. By the time we reach my house I can see she is torn between longing to come in and wanting to go home for it is late and the sun is going down and she is hungry.

'Come tomorrow,' I invite her. 'I have books with pictures you might like to see.'

Her face alight she goes skipping down the white road, pausing now and then to turn around and smile up at me; and I watch her until she is out of sight and then go home smiling to myself.

Later that evening, however, I discover that others besides myself have also noticed Tara.

'The child you met up the hill,' says Narayan suddenly, apropos of nothing in particular, 'is a clever little one. I never expected to see anyone so unusual in a village like Nekhra. Old Mahadev was also saying the same thing when I went to his shop this evening to get some rice flour.'

'What does Mahadev know about her?' Mahadev is from the hill-station, a townsman and an outsider, given to chewing betel leaves, smoking a smelly *hookah*, and uttering platitudes in a profound and unctuous tone. He runs the village shop and I can well imagine him declaiming upon the intelligence of the child ('She can count the change and calculate it in her head even faster than I can!'), punctuating his remarks by spitting the betel leaf accurately across the street from where he sits on a wooden bench at the edge of his shop.

'It is not mental arithmetic alone,' I say slowly to Narayan now. 'This child has a rare quality of mind and spirit. . . .' Narayan makes no reply but at least he does not contradict me.

After he has gone, I sit for a long while leaning against the curved back of the old easy chair, thinking of many things; watching the flames in the fireplace, the steady tawny glow of the lamp and the bronze image of Shiva throwing a fantastic shadow across the wall; listening to the crackle of pine logs and the faint tzk-tzk of the lizard on the verandah outside. No other sounds disturb the night, not even the ticking of a clock – for here in the valley time is measured only by the sun and the winds, the rain and the harvesting. There are no hurrying, dividing minutes to articulate your transience and give you the sense of something lost even before you have found it. Tonight, for me, time is an infinite awareness of living: with neither desire for a future that is uncertain, nor regret for a past that is gone; slowly I learn to hold the present in my hands and shape its fulfilment.

For my days in the village have simplicity and space. I can awaken each morning to the knowledge of a whole day waiting to be lived in – mine to mould as I please. So now, here alone in the beauty of bronze and firelight, with the mountain quietness lapping at the windows, I know I can await understanding. It will not be rushed. Maybe, when I leave this valley, I shall have decided; maybe not. Meanwhile, there is Tara. . . .

Next day, within half an hour after the school bell has clanged, she appears at my doorstep, glowing and starry with anticipation and also with having run up the hill on a full stomach.

'Why did you have to rush home for lunch and then rush back up again?' I ask her. 'You could have eaten with me.'

Her chin lifts. 'We have enough food at home.'

'I know,' I reply gently, beginning to understand that home. 'I was merely inviting you as a friend.'

She laughs and promptly forgets the incident for there are more interesting things to occupy her attention. Sitting cross-legged on the floor with the book open on her lap, turning the pages over with her delicate fingers, the child enchants me all over again with her reactions – from quick breathless exclamations to the wondering draughts of silence with which she imbibes what she sees. And then, my dear one, she finds a picture of your country. She looks at the solid, impossibly tall buildings and declares with certainty:

'Blocks. Like the ones Guruji gives to the babies' class. No one can live in those.'

'They can,' I assure her and am met with polite disbelief. 'But I have been there, Tara – look at those little dots down below on the roads. Those are people like you and me.'

She subjects me to a moment's detached, impersonal scrutiny and then decides it must be true. 'But they can't be like us if they are from a different country. They eat differently and dress differently and talk differently. Guruji told me so.'

I point out that they can think like us, however, and feel like us, but she agrees only half-heartedly. At which I find myself adding softly: 'I had friends among them, very dear friends . . .' and there is such a warmth within me, my dear one, such boundless warmth that Tara gives me another brief look and is convinced.

Then she goes back to the picture and says, 'Is it very different from your home?'

I remember her question when we first met on the hilltop. 'As different from my home, as my home is from yours. Why do you ask?'

Her eyes are suddenly sombre. 'Places are different,' she says slowly and I am left with the startled realization that this is an experienced little nomad after all.

But it is not until a couple of days later that the difference she mentions is made clearer. The bell has clanged at midday and there are no classes in the afternoon for the children have to graze their cattle on the hillside or help their parents in the fields. I can hear their shrill voices again, this time from the walnut tree below my garden; they are all gathered around it, their gaily coloured head-scarves fluttering in the breeze, lifting excited, chattering faces to the top of the tree where apparently some tree-climbing contest is in progress. Then there is an alarming creak of branches and I hear them scream 'Tara! . . .' but she manages to swing herself over to a safer branch and climbs down again, dishevelled and triumphant. I stand at my window watching them and find that it is not in this alone that Tara has to prove her audacity – she has to be the first one across the steepest, narrowest ridges; the one who balances precariously on the rickety planks bridging the ravines until she nearly falls and breaks her neck.

After this I can stand it no longer and go out to expostulate with her. But by this time she has raced halfway around the hill chasing one of the shepherd boys and only her companions are left by the

TSB Bank plc
England & Wales Division

| | | | Account number | | Sheet no. |
| | | | 6601 572471 60 | | 53 |

Date	Code	Reference	Debit	Credit	Balance
12JUL90				Brought forward	9.42
12JUL90	CHQ	097255	10.05		0.63 DR
13JUL90	CHQ	097248	4.00		4.63 DR

£50,000 FREE DRAW PLUS FINANCIAL HELP OFFERS AND ADVICE Items recently received may not be included in this statement

IN YES MAGAZINE. AVAILABLE FREE FROM YOUR TSB BRANCH.

walnut tree, swinging on its branches or sitting on the grass. They regard my approach with interest but little comment. By now I have stayed here long enough to be tolerated as an unpredictable outsider and have ceased to be a curiosity; also I am Tara's friend and my concern is understandable, if unnecessary.

'She's always like that, showing off,' says Mahadev's niece nonchalantly. 'What else can you expect from the daughter of a tribal nomad?'

Suddenly I am furious. 'Plenty,' I tell the girl sharply. 'You can expect courage, for instance, and intelligence. Ask your uncle, even he will tell you.'

But she only shrugs, unimpressed, and I realize that for a seven-year-old in a remote mountain village, Tara has enough differences and jealousies to contend with. 'My mother says it is only envy,' she explains gravely to me when we meet next. 'When I am with my mother I do not mind anything.'

I begin to respect this unknown woman tremendously, as I understand too, by piecing together fragments of information Tara gives me, something of her people. They belong to a tribe of *jhoom* cultivators – slash-and-burn agriculturists who move in hordes across the wooded Himalayan foothills, pausing before each monsoon to burn down part of the forest and grow millet, wheat or rice on the cleared land, its soil now fertile with wood-ash and rain-water. After the harvest has been gathered, they leave the charred remains behind and move on again to burn down more trees when the need arises. Obviously they are not popular with the Forest Department; and the scorn they earn from the hard-working villagers is fulsome and richly deserved. But talking to Tara, I cannot condemn this as wanton destruction, I can only accept it as a way of life. These are her people and they have something of the cruelty and splendour of their own forest fires, a casual appropriation of what the earth has to offer and a magnificent disregard of its consequences – an irresponsibility and freedom that will not be tied down by duty or need. Her immediate family too, is part of this horde even if they do not always stay with it. Sometimes they live briefly in the villages, often they trudge miles to a hill-station, for Tara's father has skill in his fingers and can carve beautiful things out of wood and stone. And her mother can give Tara a home that remains the same even if the places are different. . . . More and more, I want to meet this unknown woman, but as it turns out it is Guruji I meet next for I go to him with an idea that is forming in my mind with increasing insistence.

Guruji is every inch a village schoolmaster with inkstained clothes, glasses on the tip of his nose, bowed shoulders, and gentle smile. He welcomes me with exquisite courtesy, joining his palms in a *namaskar* of greeting; and for a moment I forget business in the sheer pleasure of being in a schoolroom like this.

The roof is thatched and the walls are washed a pure white, with windows open to the colours of the mountain and the sound of streams tumbling down the hillside like Tara's laughter, spilling into pools flecked with sunlight. Here, there is a sense not of books only, but of sky and cloud and wind and water. Our voices are quiet in this room and our words have to be honest.

'You understand of course,' says Guruji gently, 'that these people are like none you have ever known before. The way they live is because of the way they are, or maybe it is the other way around – I do not know and I have lived here too long to formulate any rules for human existence. But the fact remains that they are what is termed "wild". In Tara's family especially the pride is even more fierce, the loyalty more intense. . . .'

'I understand. And I do not want to adopt her. All I want to do is to finance her education and see that her worth isn't wasted. You know I cannot afford much, Guruji, but if she can be trained to appear for the school-leaving examinations at the hill-station, I am sure she will easily get a scholarship to the University.'

Guruji acknowledges that with his gentle smile but continues as if I had not interrupted. 'Tara's grandmother was from across the border and some say she was of royal stock. Her mother too, as you can guess, is a remarkable woman and Tara herself –' his smile broadens '– Tara is my favourite pupil. An exceptional child. I will arrange for your meeting with her parents and as far as I am concerned, I wish you well and hope your plans will succeed. But do not expect too much and do not be hurt if things don't happen the way you want them to. They may welcome your suggestion or resent it fiercely – in either case, remember you will have to tread with delicacy and tact.'

After all that, as I walk down the white road to their house the following afternoon, I cannot help viewing the approaching meeting with some trepidation. Whether by accident or arrangement, neither Tara nor her father will be home today since he has gone to a neighbouring village to sell his wares at the weekly fair, taking Tara with him. So when I finally reach the ramshackle little dwelling and climb up the wooden front steps, it is the mother alone who comes to meet me at the door.

I do not quite know what I had expected – perhaps a more mature version of Tara's loveliness – but the woman who stands before me is very much of a hill-woman. Her feet are set sturdily on the ground; her hands are broad, beautiful only because they are workworn; and the face beneath the heavy cotton veil is impassive, with slanting eyes and smooth flat contours. She utters no elaborate phrases of courtesy; but her voice is pleasant as she says quietly: 'You have been good to my daughter. Welcome to our house.'

I follow her into the wood-walled room where the older daughter is asleep, an indistinguishable hump beneath the old quilt. The mother gives her a brief glance and leads me into the kitchen where we can talk while she continues the cooking I have interrupted, squatting before the open earthen fireplace, flattening the un-leavened bread between her palms and tossing it into the fire where it puffs up for a moment on the glowing coals before it is turned swiftly over and removed, a warm golden brown. 'They generally like it hot,' she explains, 'but today I have to take my older daughter to the herb-doctor.'

I enquire after her and am told that the good herb-doctor has much healing in his hands because he has almost cured the girl and soon they will be able to leave Nekhra.

'What will happen to Tara's lessons then?' I find myself asking, forgetting to be tactful.

But her mother does not resent the question. The firelight plays across the flat planes of her face and her eyes are thoughtful.

'Nothing. She will go to school again when we come back here.'
'Will that be soon?'

'I don't know – it depends on many things. . . .' She speaks with pride of her husband's work and the flattering demand for it in the hill-station; and then with the directness so characteristic of her people, asks me where I am from and what I am doing here, whether I am married and if not, why not. I reply with equal directness that my parents have planned my engagement but await my consent, that meanwhile I have come to the valley to decide whether I should agree to that, or go back to the country where I have been studying. Her eyes widen for she cannot comprehend why I should want to return to that foreign country again, but I cannot explain about you to her, my dear one – and besides this is the opening I have been waiting for.

'Yes,' I continue, 'I am glad I came here because if I hadn't, I may never have met Tara.' And I tell her how much I admire her wisdom in handling the child and smoothing out the differences that Tara already senses so much. She makes no reply to that – I am overstepping my bounds, for this sturdy hill woman acts more from instinctive knowledge than from any theoretical precepts of child rearing. But after this, it is not too difficult to explain my plan and she listens impassively until I finish what I have to say. For a long time after I have spoken there is silence in the little kitchen. She puts away the bread and covers it to keep it warm, then turns to me and says quietly:

'Why do you think we have been away from our people so much, travelling to these villages instead of staying in the forest? It is only that Tara may be taught to read and write. My mother would have wanted it so, and Tara is very much like mother. We want it so too, her father and I. But only as much as is possible. Not too much.'

'This is not too much,' I protest in my eagerness. 'The child is brilliant and that brilliance should not be wasted.'

'Neither should her happiness,' Tara's mother replies unexpectedly. 'You spoke of the differences she feels. Those ignorant village children do that to her . . .' her voice hardens. 'Their parents are no different. We *are* different. I did not mention to you that I too can read and write, which is more than they can do. Yet I have not learned enough to make that difference too difficult to bear. But this is what you are asking for Tara – you only want to make it worse for her. When she comes back, she will never be one with her people again.'

For the first time she is definitely hostile and for the first time I can neither speak nor think, for this has gone beyond my control, beyond the immediate conflict here to an implicit one within me, constant and aching.

Her voice breaks into the agony of my thoughts with astonishing gentleness: 'What is the matter?' Sometimes the hill dialect has a strange and beautiful music to it and now it flows over my pain and gives it a meaning I can understand at last.

'I have known that difference,' I say to her, passionate with truth. 'I have known it myself and please believe me, it is worth the hurt. You have to go back to your people – you learn to suffer the difference almost gladly because then you go back with acceptance and understanding.' And I say it as much to this hill woman watching me with quiet eyes that don't quite understand my

40

vehemence, as I do to you, my dear one – for now I feel that one may be caught in conflicting rhythms but maybe one has to go back to one's own: to the hurt and strength of centuries.

'To you it may be worth it,' says Tara's mother evenly. 'But how do you know it will be worth the hardship for Tara?'

I cannot answer that; I only want to do what is best for Tara, but how can one measure the bestness – how does one *know*?

'I do not know either,' says Tara's mother. 'But we are of one mould, my daughter and I, and you are an outsider. We are a wandering people and we learn from mountains and forests – we cannot learn if we are held down to one place, not even if you give us all the books in the world. And if they are only going to make us discontented, we don't want your books, they have no meaning for us. This is our life and we know how to live it better than you do.'

Strangely enough, her tone has no hostility in it – perhaps because we both know she speaks the truth.

'Yes,' I admit slowly, more to myself than to her. 'I cannot impose the logic of my life on Tara's . . .' and the echoes hurt – they hurt and heal, remembering how once you confessed to me, half-laughing and half-serious, your constant fear that the logic of our lives might never blend even if the rest of us did. And how I laughed back and said, 'Maybe that is the best way.'

It is the inevitable working of a pattern and even as I ask Tara's mother my next question, I know her reply. For the first time since I entered her house, she smiles at me and it is a very sweet smile.

'No,' she says. 'I do not mind your seeing Tara and teaching her from your books as long as you are here. Maybe now in a short while you can give her more than you would, if you were to teach her for many years. That can happen sometimes and when it happens, it is as it should be.'

Listening to her quiet voice saying this, I realize that sometimes even what is timeless needs the duration of time to give it meaning. I think of what you and I have known, of the completeness of our experience within its particular context of time. And at last I understand the brevity of that, too, was perhaps as it should be.

For our idioms of existence are different and this is where I seem to belong, my dear one – where happiness is measured by years of human living, something you have created yourself after a lifetime of discipline, rejoicing and contentment; not something you caught as it passed and then relinquished.

'Yes,' I agree, repeating her phrase and accepting its truth. 'It is as it should be. I thank you. You have given me much.'

Still rather puzzled but smiling now beneath her heavy veil, she courteously accompanies me to the door and we part as friends.

Narayan, however, when I tell him of our interview, regards the whole episode with acute disfavour. 'You mean you wanted to take the responsibility of educating the child?'

'Yes.'

He looks at me in silence for a minute and then taps his head. 'Madness,' he diagnoses starkly. 'Sheer madness. Thank heaven that woman at least had more sense than you did.'

And there is no use after that in trying to explain my point. 'What with Narayan around,' I tell Guruji later, 'I'm sure even if I *had* been able to do something for Tara, he would have dampened whatever self-righteous glow of virtue I might have felt.'

'You probably wouldn't have felt it all,' Guruji replies with surprising shrewdness. 'One learns humility in these hills and respect for unusual values. Besides, Tara's mother would soon have taught you the difference between being charitable and being officious. A remarkable woman, isn't she? Not so much for any outstanding accomplishment as for the wisdom with which she has learned to live the life she is born to. And I think that is the most difficult education of all – even with the mountains to teach you,' he adds lightly. 'Have you had any lessons yet?'

'Yes, Guruji. I find it hard but I'm learning.' And not from the mountains alone – from you and from Narayan; from the holy man who wasn't there and from Tara who was; from Tara's mother whose decision about Tara's life helped me make a decision about mine; from the village and the days and the nights here.

Those days are turning colder around the edges now, but otherwise there is hardly any perceptible change in the tenor of village life. Every evening the women walk home from the fields singing refrains to their Moondust Mountain; and the shepherd boy's flute picks up the plaintive tune and sends it floating across the valley. Once some Tibetan peddlers come toiling up the white road behind the mule caravan. They bring ornaments of jade and turquoise and heavy hammered silver; but none in the village can afford these; so they move stolidly on towards the plains. A holy man finally appears in the cave but we do not disturb his meditation. And Tara learns her lessons and Guruji beams with pride and Narayan announces that it is time to leave the valley.

I do not protest for I know you will now understand why it is that I have made this decision to remain with my own people and accept our way of life; perhaps becoming the willing, traditional bride of the man they have chosen for me, but always hoping to find as much in my world as I pray you will find in yours.

So now for the last time I stand at my window watching the white road quiet after the goats have tinkled homewards in the twilight. There is a murmur of voices down by Mahadev's shop and in one of the wooden houses a child cries and is hushed to sleep.

It is dark now. Pine torches begin to glimmer – live golden points of light – all down the hillside. To the north the line of mountains is a faint shadow against the night sky; and beyond it range the higher Himalayas, peak after peak. In our valley the bells are stilled and our village is silent under the stars.

Appa-mam

'Mam' means uncle and the elders called him Appa, so to us he was always Appa-mam. He had other revealing epithets like 'The Shameless Rascal' and 'Old Burnt-Face' which is one of the deadlier insults in our dialect. On Appa-mam, however, it was more of a title or decoration – he wore it with such an air.

I saw him for the first time when my mother took us down to Madras to stay with my grandparents. They lived in a large, rambling house with many dark old rooms and uneven floors, overflowing with uncles and aunts and cousins and a floating population of other relatives who wandered in and stayed for a while and wandered out again. Grandfather was the Principal of a college that stood next door, so an occasional nephew or a distant third cousin who was enrolled there also sometimes came to spend the weekend – generally on his best behaviour for Grandfather's benefit.

There was one especially who, I remember thinking, was intensely romantic because he was tall and pale and had a Byronic limp from an injury which once made him faint dead away on the drawing-room carpet and lie there looking more romantic than ever. Also a part of the house was Great-grandmother, tiny and shrivelled, and senile whenever she felt like it; but always beautiful, with her snow-white hair and dark eyes, as she sat among her bedclothes and said the most amazing things. Or so it seemed to us children, though we were never allowed to hear her for very long.

Then there was Kuppu who washed clothes and cleaned vessels; she told us ghost stories and to our grandmother she recited a long string of her husband's misdemeanours, in the flat accents of the city Tamilian.

Grandmother, being gentle, sympathized with her as patiently as she listened to her mother-in-law's querulous complaints. She spoiled us and mothered her towering, six-foot sons; argued with

Grandfather, cooked divinely and expounded the Bhagavad Gita, serving us equal portions of rice and philosophy at every meal. I liked Grandfather best because he was shrewd and kind and could laugh with us or spank us at times with perfect justice. The uncles teased and the cousins could be fun. But none of them was quite as intriguing as Appa-mam.

We came in, dusty after the train journey, and found him ensconced in Grandfather's chair, wearing Grandfather's dhoti and smoking Grandfather's *bidi*. His head was clean-shaven, his forehead liberally smeared with ashes, and he was reading a newspaper.

My mother stopped short in amazement at the doorway when she saw him. 'Why, Appa-mam, when did you arrive? Where have you been all these years?'

Appa-mam smiled benignly at her. 'Ah, my child, it is always a pleasure to see you and your little ones. . . . As for myself,' he declared with dignity, 'I have been in the mountains, meditating.'

At which, one of the aunts coming in from the next room gave a very audible sniff. That was the first I knew about his having taken *sannyasa*, renouncing all worldly joys and embarking on the holy man's search for spiritual knowledge. At the moment, though, sitting in the easy chair and smoking his *bidi*, he did not look very spiritual. Nor did his subsequent behaviour prove otherwise.

Appa-mam obviously enjoyed his smoke as much as he enjoyed his sister's cooking; he insisted on helping her in the kitchen and produced all kinds of atrocious concoctions no one could eat; he had heated political discussions with my uncles, telling them stories taller than themselves; he sat in the sun and slept in the shade; he played cricket with my cousins and helped them with their algebra and they all thought it a huge joke when more than half the sums were wrong; he found the newspapers interesting and the chairs comfortable; he liked the borrowed clothes he wore and loved talking to the various assortment of relatives in the house, especially Great-grandmother. In fact I never did see anyone enjoy his life as much as this man who was supposed to have renounced all its pleasures.

He was even highly delighted by his nephews' unmerciful teasing and Grandfather's caustic comments on his *sannyasa*–hood. When the younger uncle pretended to adjust his halo, he admitted with a chuckle that it was always a little awry. And Appa-mam wasn't just being a good sport, either; he genuinely found it as funny as his nephews did and was not in the least ruffled by the aspersions cast on his holiness or the lack of it. Only once did I hear him rise to his defence and then it was with a mild, 'Well, that's *my* way of being a *sannyasi*, you know. . . .'

Appa-mam's way of being a *sannyasi*, I found later, was not only beyond definition, it was completely unpredictable. There were no rules to bind him and no ties to hold him. Sometimes he would reappear on the doorstep one fine morning with his saffron robe and begging bowl, looking thin and unshaven but as cheerful as ever. It was when you asked him where he had been that you discovered Appa-mam's creative talents. He had a different story for each person, depending on what he thought of their taste and powers of appreciation – but each version, generally, was a little wilder and more colourful than the last. Sometimes when he vanished, he took Grandfather's cuff-links with him, or maybe ten rupees from Grandmother's house-keeping money, or an odd ornament or two from the table.

This time, I heard the uncles upstairs telling each other to lock up their belongings since Appa-mam was around; and catching the implication, I sought out my mother in horror.

'Is it true Appa-mam is a thief?'

My mother sighed and said, 'Who told you that?' and when I explained, she shook her head.

'Everyone talks of his taking things but apparently no one mentions how easily he gives them away as well. Appa-mam is a peculiar sort of person, you see. Since he has taken the ascetic vow, he obviously does not believe in possessions – neither his own nor anybody else's. He wears your grandfather's clothes as if they were his own, but he himself has nothing beyond that robe and begging bowl. It's true he takes things (and you *can* call it stealing) though why he does, I wouldn't know. Anyway, whatever he takes he never keeps, it's all given away to the first needy person he comes across. Have you ever noticed anyone asking him for a smoke? He hands out not just one *bidi* but as many as he can find around. If Appa-mam had a shirt,' she finished, smiling, 'he'd probably give it proverbially off his back –'

'Then, is he a real *sannyasi*?'

'That I do not know. You'll have to judge for yourself. Though there's no point judging anyone, really, least of all Appa-mam whose standards are so entirely his own. All I can say is that if he has no compunctions about taking, he has no hesitations about giving either.'

As if to prove her point, the next day Appa-mam announced that he was going on foot to the temple at Tirukazhukunram, to make a day's pilgrimage and return by nightfall. Grandmother got up at dawn to cook some rice for him and packed it carefully into a bell-metal lunch container that had belonged to their father. Younger uncle, who was also up early that morning studying for an examination, watched Appa-mam depart and then turned to his mother.

'I don't mind if the Old Burnt-Face doesn't return,' he remarked with a heartless grin, 'but I certainly hope that the lunch container does.'

Late that evening, however, the Old Burnt-Face did return – a weary, footsore, bedraggled object in the dusk – bearing the empty container with him. He was so exhausted that he could hardly talk but managed nonetheless to remark with his usual dignity that these few days of soft living had spoiled him for even a single day of starvation.

'Starvation?' Grandmother echoed incredulously. 'But I packed the lunch for you myself!'

Appa-mam dismissed that with a wave of his hand. 'Oh, I know, there was plenty of rice and there was another pilgrim on the way who hadn't eaten for two days, so I gave it to him. But I remembered to ask for the container back,' he added with justifiable pride. 'I remembered that you liked it.'

'It was Father's,' Grandmother said in a small voice. But Appa-mam had already forgotten the whole episode and was half way up the stairs, mumbling between yawns that he wanted to have his bath and dinner and get to sleep as soon as possible.

'Don't have any nightmares,' Grandfather called after him, and everybody roared.

Appa-mam's nightmare was part of the family legend that was later to accrue around him. His previous visit had been rather a long one. No one had seen him for three years and then one night when the boys were away at college and my grandparents had gone early to bed, a dark figure appeared at the gate calling hoarsely: 'Premavati! Premavati!' . . . My grandmother woke up with a start at hearing her name and was terrified for a moment until

Grandfather woke up too and saw who it was and said, 'Oh, you Old Burnt-Face, have you come back again?'

Appa-mam had not only come back, he had even brought with him the twenty-five rupees he had taken from Grandfather's desk during his last visit. The uncles decided later that it was probably this extreme act of virtue which brought on the nightmare. Whatever the cause, the fact remained that Grandfather woke up at midnight to find Appa-mam yelling some gibberish and dancing like a dervish around his bed.

'Appa,' he said sharply, 'stop it. What do you think you're doing, waking everybody at this time of night?' But Appa-mam continued to yell and wave his arms and dance around the bed.

'Appa,' Grandfather said louder. 'Appa, stop it!'

Even that had no effect, so he finally got up and gave Appa-mam a resounding thrash on his back. At that, Appa-mam stopped abruptly, sat down on the bed and opened his eyes; and Grandfather discovered the man had been asleep all the time.

'Good God, I might have killed you! – what on earth were you doing?'

Appa-mam sat and looked at Grandfather in silence, thinking of an explanation. Eventually he found it. 'Cats,' he said. 'That's what it was. You don't keep cats.' And he went back to bed.

He never heard the end of that and neither did we.

There was a new game in the family after this, evolved by the youngest generation and called Appa-mam's Nightmare – with one playing Grandfather, the other taking Appa-mam's role, and the smallest being the cats that weren't.

Listening to that story, I had felt vaguely sorry for Appa-mam for having nightmares; but (apart from the fact that he did not seem to be afflicted by them any more) seeing him now, it was as difficult to pity as it was to condemn him. And though I still could not decide about his identity as a real *sannyasi*, it was equally difficult to make an enigma out of him. He continued to be Appa-mam: cheerful and happy-go-lucky, unconcerned about any of the things that worried other grown-ups, and deriving an immense satisfaction out of just being alive.

And then one day the disciples came. Kuppu saw them first: a motley collection of people peering in, dubiously, at the gate, wanting to know if the *sannyasi* was at home, and if they might obtain his *darshan*, his personal blessing. She brought the news to us at breakfast, all agog with excitement.

Appa-mam swallowed his coffee and said with composure, 'Ah yes, my disciples.'

'Your disciples!' grandmother exclaimed. 'We didn't know you had any!'

It was only then we learned that Appa-mam really *had* been practising silent meditation for years, near a little North Indian village where he had acquired a band of devotees and been revered as a saint.

The older uncle, who was an economist and the most irreverent of us all, was the first to recover from this dumbfounding bit of information.

'I had always suspected,' he said, 'that half these holy men were a bunch of charlatans. Now I know for certain. Imagine anyone coming to seek Appa-mam's *darshan* –'

And the younger uncle ruminated aloud that he might as well leave the Law College and become a *sannyasi*, since it seemed to be a much more profitable occupation. A cousin choked over the *idli* he was eating, and soon the aunts had begun to giggle and everyone thought it was the funniest thing that had happened in years.

Meanwhile Appa-mam finished his breakfast quite undisturbed by the general amusement and all the derogatory comments flying back and forth. Then finally he spoke, and his voice – Appa-mam's familiar, cheerfully raucous voice – was more quiet than we had ever heard it.

'Understand this,' he said. 'I have no objection to your laughing about it all. But if you have a grain of sense in your heads, don't do that in front of the disciples. Once they have gone you can laugh at me as much as you like, it will make no difference. But while they are here, remember they have come a long way and respect their faith.'

The laughter died down and there was quiet after that. Having performed the necessary rites of purification and worship Appa-mam sat cross-legged under the neem tree at the back of the house and saw his disciples one by one.

They came walking across the courtyard (a mother with her baby, an old farmer, a cripple, a young couple, a handful of children), all of them bringing offerings of milk and coconuts and wild honey and rice. Appa-mam blessed each of them, especially the little ones, made the cripple sit next to him and rest awhile, spoke to the farmer and smiled at the young couple with a gentle benediction that none of us – watching fascinated from kitchen window – had ever seen before.

That night, after the devotees had left and Appa-man had come in, when everybody had gone to bed and the house was silent, I mentioned to my mother that I had decided Appa-mam was a real *sannyasi* after all.

Two days later, my aunt's earrings were missing and so was Appa-mam. We have not heard of him since.

Monologue for Foreigners

Who are you, sitting there across the table? Oh yes, of course you turn your head when your name is called and we answer obediently to ours, my twin and I. But that's not the point: it never is, is it? Your name merely announces you are a foreigner to us as our clothes declare we are foreigners to you, your land, and most of all to these seedy little hang-outs that mushroom across the backways of North America.

The very airlessness is blue here like that neon tube overhead which shimmers across the ice cubes tinkling in our glasses, outlines the light and dark bodies around us, and spills over you sitting there deliberately dissolute: face reddened with drink, tie askew and hair tumbled over your damp forehead – very expert as your eyes appraise the girl dancing in the tinsel cage above us.

I've seen it all, says that look of yours, like every one of your stories. I've drunk till dawn with Prince Soandso; smooched genteelly in the bathtub with Lady Thisandthat; plucked ylang-ylang blossoms, eaten mangosteens, gone courting and carousing from Lapland to Tasmania, Tikal to Angkor Wat. I've known him; I've loved her; I've been there. . . . Fact? Fantasy? Does it make any difference? You make us laugh, they way you flick glances of sidelong lechery at the dancer when she steps down from the cage and slithers into her chair at the next table. Portrait of a Rake with overtones: for all the vaunted ranges of your past, you take things in so ingenuously: life to be washed down with endless bottles of Scotch, some slight alarm and that saving sense of humour. You're terribly funny – you know?

Something about the slow, slurred, slightly stammering speech with which the lines are delivered. You seem to laugh, drink, live, not only because you have to but with the triumphant knowledge that you still care to. . . .

What did she say? The music blares so loud, you can't hear anybody around this table. Yes, undoubtedly; it's the perpetual human condition. So listen: since you safely cannot hear us, we can talk to you. As you see we belong to a brown-skinned race, recognize a kinship with the dark people among us, like the dancer above. The dark of prejudice, that is, not the tan of privilege. Though heaven knows our own people are prejudiced enough.

In the hills above our home when we lived near the northeast frontier, the tribesmen told their story of the creation of man. In the beginning God prepared the dough and set it to cook. First, He left it too long, and it came out overdone: thus the black man happened in Africa. Then He got unduly cautious and removed the dough before it was quite ready; thus the white man happened in Europe. The third time, at last perfect with practice, He managed to cook man just right, not too long, not too little – and out *we* came in Asia: not too dark, not too light, the exact toasted brown He had wanted all along. . . . So you see?

Day before yesterday, standing in line before us at lunch, you said: 'The only way to take life is to laugh it out of countenance.' How can one help laughing at such a legend, especially when we stand willy-nilly with the rest of mankind on both sides of that myth, sinning and sinned against? – Yet rejoicing mainly in the irrelevance of moments like this one now: when this world's clamour only makes silence clearer, its prejudices strip away our skin, its labels and advertisements cancel our names entirely and allow us all to come together unclaimed like pieces of stranded luggage – world people matching difference to sameness: nothing else.

For instance, we once lived for a while in your island sanctuary on the Atlantic coast. Grew to love the long low line of its beach and marshes, the milky sheen of its light on certain mornings, its houses perched like crabs along rocks and the tremendous strength of that ocean all round beating its people against one another. 'M-makes them insular,' was all you said, unimpressed.

But it was different on *our* island sanctuary, perhaps because that was Greek and on the Aegean Sea. A pair of dispossessed travellers, we had stumbled on it in passing but ended up staying a whole year. There Tassos painted his boat all day long, all the spring long: vermilion around the sides, cobalt blue on deck, with oars of an unabashed yellow. . . . Patches of snow left over from winter melted handful by handful into rivulets trickling down rocks; flowers bloomed wild all over the hillsides: lupins as blue as his deck, splendour of sorrel as gold as his oars. 'In three weeks maybe

I launch my boat.' 'In a week –' 'Tomorrow. . . .' 'What time?' He looked around at our circle of eager faces and then up into the answering blue to weigh the sky, the sea, the promise of wind. 'Three o'clock in the afternoon.' But by one-thirty, well before we few outsiders could gather at the harbour, he had collected a couple of his old cronies, they put gnarled hands and shoulders against the orange pained wood and pushed his lovely *Kore* into the bay. He had to keep his moment private and auspicious with old friends; we were friends too, but too new: neither tried like his boat nor weathered like the shingle of your houses along the Atlantic.

Your islanders are like our islanders in that respect: you are as foreign to your sanctuary as we were to ours. Yet your island itself stays insistently different, very restrained and Anglo-Saxon in the muted tones of its landscape, the tenuous quality of its light – so unlike the Aegean clarity and resplendence of ours.

We especially counted those Greek sunsets, like a secular rosary, for peace and concentration: dark hill still against the sky; grey silk sea; afterlight of gold and paler gold; one star . . . And do you know, in daylight our eyes were so smitten by the colour of the sea that all the shadows on the island turned blue? Everywhere. On sun-dazzled wheat fields, on dovecotes, on houses square and white and simple like so many sugar cubes.

Ah, to describe our island properly we need white plaster instead of words – and water and sky and the deep wild colours of the mountainside with which to spell our days and nights there. . . . Perhaps in our wanderings one day we three will meet inside a sugar-cube house and sit and talk together; but I suspect there might be nothing to say.

I beg your pardon? A cigarette? Certainly. Here – In the business of lighting it, the woman next to you suddenly begins to play the almost-touching game: a brush of hands, a whiff of perfumed skin tantalisingly close. Already, in the space of an evening, those unclaimed edges of our selves are starting to blur; the currents that wash around this table will inevitably turn us all into social appendages of one another: 'OW!' says the woman next to you, slapping an unlikely mosquito and throwing herself about. She has become the prime joke at the summer job where we all happen to find ourselves – a mixed assortment in one enormous old country house.

They call her The Chaser and soon will watch, amused, as she pursues you indefatigably up to the roof and down to the garden while you back away slightly . . . and keep backing away until the day before your or her scheduled departure. At which point, when there is no danger of subsequence, you will climb into your car and drive slowly around under the elms and pick her up at the back door. So many rooms and hotels to rent in this holiday town; any one should do. Then you will drive back in the evening, face more flushed than ever, loosen your tie, rumple your hair, and have four more drinks than usual because the role of a Rake Satisfied leaves you rather at a loose end.

For naturally this is just one of many poses – Sketch of the Artist's Son being the hardest to outgrow. 'We weren't very close,' you remarked one day and clammed up at once as if appalled at your lack of reticence. But pictures come through in phrases as well as on canvas: phrases unconsciously dropped that paint a home not so much broken as indifferent. You, small, floundering, almost drowned in the silence between a nonentity of a mother and far too famous father (idol plus *bête noire* in one, whose shadow you still can't escape) are shunted off to a succession of very exclusive schools, each – to hear you tell it – grisly enough to make Orwell's account sound like a parlour game. What precisely overtook you there is anybody's guess.

Your eyelid twitches sometimes and you can't sit for long in any one place without hitching your chair a little further away, turning half-around to see what's going on elsewhere: loth to commit yourself even to the edge of a convivial table. We can imagine you similarly pushing your place back and away from personal relationships. Somewhere, sometime, there have been wives – yesterday you mentioned the undivorced one who was revealed between the lines as a selfish, scampering little cat.

No change in your raconteur's tone when you describe that; it's just another anecdote slipped in among the rest. But then there is a child too. And with his birth is born your terror, haltingly confessed, lest your childhood miseries be perpetuated all over again on his infinitely precious head. None of us can reassure you about that. There's no way to relieve the humbled, nonplussed look you wear when you realize you have a son, and that even if you hitch your chair two steps away from the sweetness and agony of relationship, he continues relentlessly to be your child. For in your book a wife after all may be detachable; but a son, like a father, is not.

After about the third glass or so must rise the memory of his small and crumpled face being handed gingerly back into the starchy arms of a hospital nurse. 'L-looks about a hundred years old, doesn't he? Ugly little mugger!' The usual mumbling inarticulacies. . . . Yet logical that in a moment like this, the rake as well as the raconteur should vanish, reducing you to a bone of human truth.

And what of her, the woman against the pillows? Whatever her quality, even when you connect her casually with the child you grant her the grandeur and continuity of generations – for all the world like that Athenian tomb stele of Ampherete and her grandchild, which inscribes their bond so freshly down two thousand three hundred years of living and dying. How does it go? 'I am holding here the child of my daughter, the beloved, whom I held on my lap when, alive, we beheld the light of the sun; and now I am holding it dead, being dead myself.'

A lull between numbers. Someone gets up to order another round of drinks, someone else disappears into the bathroom. The music sets up again and dancers jam together on the minuscule floor. In the reshuffling of places we find you suddenly beside us. It is the time of night when tongues are traditionally loosened: 'Women,' you mutter, the way fools find scapegoats. 'Demanding, asserting, badgering all the time. Can't leave a f-fellow alone.' Nothing to do with The Chaser, this, even if you recover yourself enough to glance fleetingly as if in illustration at her gyrating among the rest.

Behind your eyes is an image of heaven knows how many females playing tug-of-war, each grown monstrous in the process: billowing like comic-strip balloons over your hapless and hunted head. The saxophone slices between us, damming further talk. My twin and I turn to each other, smiles fading, as we remember an old friend at home agitating in Parliament for the passing of divorce laws; of the unbearable statistics quoted then: one suicide a day, 365 a year, in Saurashtra alone, by women caught in cruel marriages with no escape at all, no corner to hide from the neglect or sadism of husbands and the constant swarming venom of relatives – impossible to count how many daughters-in-law are daily beaten, starved, hounded to their death in one way or another. Our people can be bound to suffocation by families; yours as ruthlessly torn apart.

No, life carries no simultaneous equations really, only this matching of difference to sameness, fragment – sometimes, as now, in utter futility because friendships like everything else can get too complicated: we cannot reach across, heal, and take a touchstone strength from one another as we were taught on the Greek island.

One night, soon after the boat had been launched. Tassos took us
up to celebrate a festival – a *panagyri* – at his church which stood
whitewashed and luminous, as if hewn out of solid moonlight, on
the crown of a hill.

We ascended into white on white: white stone steps leading up,
white stone benches built into the walls all around, a low wooden
table truly groaning with food and topped by jugs and jars and
bottles of white wine: tart, tawny and homemade. Tassos got drunk
that night, playing his goatskin *tsambouna* which swelled and
sounded exactly like bagpipes – drunk; drunker; magnificent with
wine and music and friendship as only three or four of us were
finally left, dancing in a circle on the hillside under the stars,
whipped by the wind, touching and teetering across white stones
and dark night, knowing that as the wind swept our skin darkness
could sweep our world, blotting it out. All the more important then
to snatch friendship in the teeth of that dark, and touch each other
with love, only that contact saving us, saving us, as we danced and
slithered down the dark hill, the stars entangled in our hair, the sea
our very anklet.

This dancing here: what can we or any polite foreigners say,
except 'How different!'? Neither years of classical discipline nor the
glory of a night in spring. No sea or stars or myths to burn your body
here; only flight from original sin, perhaps, a crumbling sense of
avowal and disavowal (is this your own malaise?) and many funny
antics to hide the inner fear, the all too dreary guilt. Really to
dance, as to love or laugh or grieve, is in a way to say yes. Not this,
is it? – brightly vigorously nodding while a terrified child screams
'No! No! No!' inside your skull.

*No, no, no. Thank you, I can't dance this. . . . What am I giggling
about? Nothing really.* Just echoes. Contradictions. *Oh hello! Look
who's here.* You grin, blinking and peering up at the newcomer, a
sweet and sturdy-boned farm lass who is the latest addition to our
menage in the big house. Remote so far, she now immediately
provokes your interest by hanging on to another man's arm. All the
signs are hung out at once: rivalry, impediment, pursuit and retreat
– a series of skirmishes planned by the various nuances of the flesh
and played out to a final rendezvouz which you will keep with
customary *élan* and one eye on the escape hatch.

But first, after a suitably discreet interval, you ask her to dance. The Chaser begins to bristle at this, makes overtures to the farm girl's escort and is pallidly rejected. So, out of some old-world sense of courtesy and obligation, you dance with her as well and perpetrate triangles that form and break and form again, fraught with all the delicate tensions of a preamble.

Soon however the music gets faster, more frantic: the room hotter; mannerisms accentuated. The gestures of the girl acquire an angular freshness, she speaks less and less. On the other hand, The Chaser's very flesh grows voluble; even as we watch she turns perceptibly more buxom. All the inconsequence of a flirtation is belied by these smoky lights and rhythms; every movement becomes part of an unmistakable choreography. At this you take fright and return to our table.

However once you are headed for a crescendo you have to see it through – don't you know that by now? – and here the most beautiful of the dancers steps in. The delicate bones of her face, its subtly exquisite texture and colouring reminds me of my twin's; though there the resemblance ends. Making her sinuous way to the cage, she lingers by your chair and breathes invitingly: 'C'mon up and dance with me, baby?'

'Any time,' you leer, never at a loss. 'Any time, soon as all these people leave.' But when she moves on, you raise flailing arms across your face, fending her off and cowering away in mock horror. 'G-good God! I've never been unfaithful, not once in fifteen years. How can she expect me to do a thing like that?'

Before the laughter at your extravagance and duplicity has died down, and while the dancer is still climbing up to the cage she stumbles on the last step and falls. With a flash of lovely sequinned legs and a thud, her body hits the floor. There is a moment of frozen silence; nobody moves.

Then in the stillness a chair scrapes. You are running to her side and kneeling down to help. The silence, instead of breaking, intensifies to a strange double whisper of movement. The blurred white faces at the table turn instinctively to the dark ones behind the bar. There someone responds, swaying muffled and sullen: 'Hey –' I am conscious of moving with both, afraid on one side and angry on the other; split; helpless as the girl who lies there looking like my twin. It has all taken just a moment but that moment too is split: first shock, then the little prickle of warning – race riots; take-your-hands-off-that-girl; fear.

Endless, endless; but only for that split second. Suddenly, in the incalculable way of things, it's over. The dancer smiles and sits up. Hands and voices resume their function. You return to our table.

'You drop out of Med School or something?' The Chaser enquires.

'First aid,' you mumble. 'Just first aid.' And we see again the moment when all your poses absented themselves: as you tended the girl with that willingness and certainty which comes not from any professional deftness but a pure and uninflected human concern. In the end, impaled by necessity, you will commit yourself to anyone who can't reciprocate.

'You had us scared there for a minute,' somebody else says. 'This is quite a neighbourhood, in case you didn't know –' which evokes another embarrassed mumble, this time to be passed off as a jest in ultracultivated accents: 'Well, one is doomed to be a gentleman, you know, and all that . . .'

Yes. And many-a-true-word and all that, too. However much you may run from it, there it is, that gentleman's code of yours, waiting inexorably to rein you in, straighten your back, and coerce you into doing the right thing.

As the waiter brings the check, conversation subsides in eddies around the table. We can no longer ask: What do you really seek behind the predictable disguises of liquor and women when you flee your background and, fooling us for a moment, claim yourself a wanderer like us? Forgive us, we had no right. That you give bits of yourself away in event and anecdote doesn't absolve us in the least. Neither does our affection and regard for you. But we wanderers have our obsessions too, you see.

Disguised by the need to know what makes a person tick, we constantly seek islands of discovery and recognition in other people – setting our compass only by that fragmented overlap of difference to sameness. We have inherited too many worlds: our senses reach back for landscapes known and remembered but our roots lie only in our imagination and among those we love. Hence that child inside our skull who insists on begging: Are you perhaps one of them? Will you perhaps prove a friend?

Very soon we will leave this table, this town, this country, and scatter again, broadcast to the wind. When we get up, the garish neon overhead dissolves our skin into a streaky and multicoloured palette as if, outside crisis, we can at most merely exchange our patches of fool's motley: making gestures appropriate and inappropriate; taking shreds, moments and half-sentences home for comfort.

Outside the night is a clear burnished black and gold. Some who have indulged less stagger more. You maintain a steady pace, and light your cigarette with an equally steady hand. We walk together and apart, all of us, carving our brief share of space above the pavement. No steles mark our habitation – no inscription at all on a stone or a table or a sugar-cube house, not even in the faint curling smell of a single cigarette drifting up from an empty street at midnight – to say we have been and gone.

Too Late for Anger

My sister always said the crockery in the Kirit household smelled of eggs. The Kirit sisters smelled, too, but of perfume – heavy and overpowering perfume, perhaps logically, since they were heavy and overpowering themselves. The brothers reeked of tobacco, occasionally of liquor. And the last time I visited them there was another smell, the most disturbing of all – a dank odour of decay that carried with it the echoing footsteps of the only two Kirits now left in the old house.

We had known the Kirits, as I will call them, as far back as I can remember. They were family friends – the eldest brother, Raj, a colleague of my father's; and the youngest sister, Lena, already a teacher while I was still in middle school. The father had been a doctor. Old Man Kirit, he was called, a familiar and well-loved figure in the south. His rise had been phenomenal. He came from a family of fisherfolk on the west coast – a penniless youth arriving in the city, working his way through night school and then the medical college, winning scholarships, gathering friends along with degrees, marrying a clever, ambitious, 'useful' wife, whom he loved, and buying a big house in what had been the most exclusive section of Madras.

When I saw it one day last year, buses rumbled past, jostled by rickshaws and clattering horse-drawn jutkas; there were big shops and little wayside stalls selling betel leaves and spices, and always the hurrying thrum of humanity on the pavements. But the house was set well back from the road and the noises were muffled, caught between the close-leaved branches of the tamarind trees that lined the drive and somehow sheltered the big house and what it held. That day, I found the garden lying shrivelled and bare. The drive was ill-kept, a few flowerpots wilted on the front steps, and the halls and rooms seemed to be furnished with spaces – unyielding, tangible spaces that told you they had once been filled.

63

The floor, too; beneath the dust, the marble mosaic gleamed dully, of better times, when the mother had insisted on its being swept and washed twice a day. Her portrait (painted when she was still a middle-aged woman) hung on the wall of the living room – a sombre thing of greys and greens merging into vague surrounding blackness. Yet the dark did not overshadow her, dominate her; instead, it was as if she created the dark. I shivered a little, looking at it, and wondered how well the artist had known her. How could he have sensed the darkening when the house was full of sunlight? When the daughters were young and beautiful and the sons reputedly brilliant and sought-after? Raj and Jairaj, slapping their tennis rackets across their knees, running down the stairs laughing. And the girls with their floating pastel saris, their absurdly rhyming names: Meena and Nina and Lena. The only odd one out had been Sheela. She was slight and dark and quiet, painfully conscious of the cast in her left eye, a shadow behind her mother, helping to run the house, supervise in the kitchen, see to the meals. We never saw her with the others at picnics and parties and concerts – not even in the library or on the beach. She always stayed behind, a silent, soft-footed wraith moving through the empty rooms when the others had gone out. My sister and I called her Cinderella and thought it a pity that Madras was too warm for fires. She would have made a perfect picture sweeping the hearth. And besides, it would be fun playing fairy godmother to her, devising ways to transform her into a vision of grace.

We pitied her with the extravagant loyalty of youth, but never thought to pity the others. Weren't they forever going out, enjoying themselves, walking the earth like large and beautiful goddesses in their exquisite clothes? We never realized that they were always formidably flanked by their parents – the mother grim and compelling (her daughters must always have the best) and the father booming pleasantries left and right, thumping people on the back, being thumped in return. We didn't know until years later their almost neurotic fear of being talked about. They were the Kirit girls and they had to remain pure and lovely, untouched alike by rumour or the bazaar smells that were already beginning to creep into the gracious neighbourhood.

Meena was the eldest of the girls, the most slender and serene. Her friends called her the Waiting Madonna, because her dreamy dark eyes always seemed to be fixed on Wednesday week – or any other day in the middle distance, towards which she poised her whole being and even pitched the tone of her voice, low but carrying. But whatever it was she was waiting for was large enough to include her immediate surroundings in its direction; if you happened to be in her line of vision, she noticed you, was exquisitely courteous and attentive, and acquired the reputation of being a wonderful hostess. Yet there remained the remoteness, the waiting, and it made her a strangely restful person to be with. When she and Lena graduated from the university with honours and prepared to leave for England, we thought she had come to what she was waiting for: travel, education, widening perspectives – all that a trip abroad held. They were away three years, Lena reading English at Oxford. Meena at the London School of Economics. What those three years did for them I do not know; presumably, what study abroad does for most Indian youth. If they developed the intellectual schizophrenia that afflicts Westernized Easterners, or found it difficult to fit into their appointed niches as daughters of the family when they returned, they did not show it. And Meena still waited.

Meanwhile, the other sister, Nina, had enrolled in the local medical college, riding on the wave of her father's success but proving herself adequately bright and more than adequately attractive. 'Carries on the tradition, eh?' Old Man Kirit boomed, hugely pleased. He took her with him everywhere he went, while Sheela stayed at home, depending more and more on her mother, shrinking away from all other human contact.

'It isn't *good* for her,' Raj said to us, roused out of his usual cheerful imperturbability. 'I worry about her. I worry terribly.' Raj was closest to us, meeting us most often and discussing his problems with my parents. He didn't look worried. Raj had inherited his father's bonhomie, claiming to be waiting for my sister and me to grow up so he could marry one or the other of us. 'Give me Mangalore girls every time, hey?' he would say, pinching my cheek. 'Famous for two things, Mangalore: the splendour of its landscape and the beauty of its women.' We wished we weren't from Mangalore, but smiled politely and agreed in private that he was being rather ridiculous, constantly talking about the pretty girls he would like to marry.

As it turned out, Raj never married. Within a few months after the girls returned to India, Old Man Kirit and his wife were killed in a motor accident. When my mother came home from the funeral, I heard her say, 'This will break poor Sheela unless the rest of them rally around her. Already she looks like death.' And my father replied, abruptly for him, 'They've always been close – I hope they get more independent now.' But the Kirits only grew closer still.

Raj postponed marriage. First, the girls had to be married, 'settled'. The responsibility devolved upon him as the eldest, and besides, Jairaj, after the prescribed period of mourning, was too busy being a playboy. He joined a foreign business firm, spent his Saturday afternoons at the racecourse, threw himself with éclat into the cocktail-party crowd, and took to drinking a good deal. 'Women, too,' the gossips muttered darkly. Whether that was prompted by malice or fact, Jairaj was undoubtedly attractive to women. A shooting accident that injured his leg had left him with a limp; he rode and swam well, and could be articulate in a brittle fashion that passed for wit. 'Stands there blowing cigarette smoke in your face and raising his left eyebrow, and the girls fall for it every time,' Raj reported gloomily. 'Romantic as hell.'

Soon after this, Jairaj offered the tentative suggestion that he take a flat in town, but the idea evaporated of its own accord. Perhaps the dead mother's disapproval glaring down at him from the wall or his own guilt at deserting the family proved too strong. And he was comfortable enough in the big house; Raj was an easygoing head of the family, making no demands on the others, only upon himself.

The girls were working now. Meena and Leena became decorative additions to the staff of a women's college, and Nina an intern in the city's new hospital. But it was tacitly agreed that this state of affairs was temporary. Career women were still something out of the ordinary, and the Kirit girls were avid for the conventional, the 'safe' life – a placid marriage and then an inevitable family strongly bulwarked by the oh-so-solid social structure. They came home straight from work, to avoid the least breath of scandal, for girls who acquired the wrong kind of reputation rarely acquired the right kind of husband.

And then there was Sheela. Lovingly and slowly, her brothers and sisters tried to chip off the layers of numbness that enveloped her. Listlessly, she allowed them to do what they liked. They took her to concerts and parties and the theatre, but she endured each as if it were an infliction rather than an entertainment. They brought her plenty to read, but she sat at the window, gazing out, with the book lying open and unread on her lap. They took her shopping and bought her fashionable ensembles, but the new clothes looked

66

vaguely apologetic on Sheela, as if they were begging her pardon for being there.

'I don't know *what* to do with the girl,' Raj finally complained to my mother, in desperation. 'Nothing seems to work. *She* won't work, either. Or study.'

My mother thought for a moment and then said, with apparent irrelevance, 'How about the Temple Festival at Shivanur? We're going – would you like to join us?'

So we all went together.

Shivanur is a seacoast village about thirty miles south of Madras. Every twelve years, pilgrims from all over the country gather there to attend its famous Temple Festival. The temple itself stands on the seashore, where the sea and the sculptured stone have been looking at each other for the last fifteen hundred years. Legend has it that the Ganga, flowing through a secret underground source, joins the sea here once in twelve years. Then prayers are said at dawn and the pilgrims bathe in the sea; the ritual worship of puja is performed in the temple and the poor are fed.

All day the village is alive with the temple fair. We saw potters with their earthenware, farmers with their grain, bangle sellers, little boys selling baskets, whole families of weavers squatting behind the vivid silks flung enticingly across their stalls to attract the pilgrims. There were trinkets for women and brightly painted wooden toys for children, and the objects used for worship – beautiful old lamps and bells, rosaries made of dried *rudrakshi* berries, the sacred texts bound in cloth, fruits and flowers, sandalwood, camphor, and incense.

The Kirit women, grown up as they were, seemed almost as excited as my sister and I. They bought us some glass bangles, and when the bangle seller slipped the tinkling blues and greens on our wrists, Meena tried them on too, quoting Sarojini Naidu's poem about 'rainbow-tinted circles of delight'. Nina lost herself in the silk shops, to emerge half an hour later with shimmering folds of tangerine and gold, but Lena could not buy anything, because she had given away all her money to the beggars who throng every Hindu place of pilgrimage. And apparently my mother had known what she was talking about, for here at last Sheela came to life – slowly at first, until she worshipped at the temple and mingled with the crowds at the fair, caught in a throbbing, insistent new rhythm so utterly unlike the measured pace of existence in the big house that she surrendered in spite of herself.

'I'd like to come here when all the people have left,' Meena announced suddenly. We were drinking tender-coconut milk on the beach beside the temple courtyard. 'I'd like to live here always. Just sketch and bathe and be; lie on the sands or here in the shade of the temple, listening to the wind in the palms, soaking in *centuries* of peace. And live on tender-coconuts all day.' Jairaj murmured something cynical about indigestion, but she wasn't listening. She turned to her older brother and her eyes were suddenly brilliant. 'Raj, I've decided,' she said. 'It's yes.'

That was how we knew that Raj's efforts at hunting for a brother-in-law had proved successful. 'The boy,' as everyone referred to him, was pronounced entirely satisfactory. He was from the same linguistic community, had completed his education abroad and so did not mind a 'foreign-returned' bride with more academic degrees than was seemly for a woman; also, he was a pilot in the Air Force, suitably dashing and suitably well connected. Meena had met him twice. 'You know,' she admitted later, 'It does become rather an impasse in this society of ours. You can't get engaged to a person until you know him well enough, and you can't know him well enough until you get engaged to him. Anyway, I've decided as best I could under the circumstances . . .' and her eyes were brilliant again.

Watching Meena in those days was almost frightening. Her radiance had a perilous edge. She was so beautiful that you couldn't look at her for long; you turned away from the naked joy in her eyes. Now Meena had no more need to wait.

Her fiancé stayed in Madras for a week and then went north for special military training. Raj kept congratulating himself on his success and consulting my mother about preparations to be made for the wedding. Meena's horoscope was sent to the astrologer, and word came back that the wedding would have to be postponed for six months, since both 'the boy' and 'the girl' were passing through what he called 'an uncertain period'. Meena herself, seeming not the slightest bit uncertain, went shopping for her trousseau with her sisters.

But it was only Sheela she took with her on the trip to the silk weavers' town, where saris were cheaper than in the city. It rained that weekend, and both girls were drenched and came home with colds which worsened to a serious chill, spelling pleurisy. Meena, being the stronger of the two, was recovering slowly, but Sheela grew thin and feverish and bright-eyed, and before the end of the month Raj brought bad news. Her lungs were badly affected; the doctors said she had to be removed to a sanatorium.

What came next happened with bewildering rapidity. Sheela was moved to the sanatorium, and a week later Meena's engagement was broken by her fiancé's family. With tuberculosis in the family, they said, You Never Know.

Raj came to us with haggard eyes. 'I haven't told her yet,' he said. 'I couldn't. Not when she's ill. And she keeps waiting for the mail and wondering why there are no letters. . . .'

'But *why*?' my sister cried indignantly. She had always loved Meena best. 'Why should they do a thing like that? Illness isn't a crime –'

'Here it apparently is,' Raj replied bitterly. 'Marriage is a breeding institution, and they want to make sure the production machine is in working order.' We had never seen him so angry.

'And what about *him*?' we persisted, almost equally angry. 'Why doesn't *he* do something about it? He loved – well, *liked* her, didn't he?'

Raj stopped us with a gesture. 'Because he hasn't the guts. Because our country today breeds namby-pamby Milquetoasts, with neither the discipline of the old nor the vigour of the new – they haven't the faith to live with duty and haven't the courage to live without it. They're a living celebration of the apron string.'

'And Meena?'

'I don't know – this sort of thing pretty well shuts up all other avenues. She's caught in the same chasm between the old and the new. Our girls are given the education and ideals to believe in freedom, but never the circumstances and encouragement to carry it out, to live what they believe. It's a sham all around . . .' He paused in his tirade and then touched my cheek gently. 'You, too, little ones. Perhaps the next generation will escape – but you'll get it. And my other sisters, God knows what will happen to them.'

Soon he did know. Lena, watching the tragic, empty-eyed shell of a human being that Meena had become, announced that she would have none of these arranged marriages if this was the way they ended. And, trying to shake off the old dread of being talked about, she joined a group of teachers who were taking a trip to Kashmir during the summer vacation. Our family had moved north that summer, so we saw her on her way back. She was with another professor, a thin, eager, dark man with restless hands, a voluble tongue, and the high intellectual forehead of the South-Indian Brahman. They came to tea and he talked all the time, handling abstract concepts as palpably as he handled the cup in his hand. Lena looked and smiled and listened, and then, just before they left, she drew my mother aside with a swift, shy gesture unexpectedly touching in someone with her usual assurance. They hoped to be married when they returned to Madras, she said, after Gopal's parents had given their permission and blessing.

There was no blessing. We heard about the scene later. The father had raged and stamped and threatened to throw his son out of the house. The mother had cowered and wept in a corner. 'Marry a girl from the fisher-people!' he had roared, his sacred thread quivering in indignation, the caste mark on his forehead drawn together in a thunderous frown. 'How *dare* you pollute the air in this house with a blasphemous suggestion like that –' It was all rather like the classic situation in one of our third-rate films, we thought. Of course, the young intellectual would walk out of the house and marry the girl he loved.

We waited – the mother had begged for time. And the father used it. Barely a week later, Gopal was told that he was to be married to a remote cousin thrice removed, a wellborn young woman with no highfalutin foreign ideas and no more education than was good for her. It was all arranged; the date had been set, down to the auspicious moment when he would clasp wedding *tali* around the girl's neck, and the invitations had already been sent out. It was too late to change anything. If Gopal did, it would spell disaster not only to the girl but to the entire clan. They would never live down the disgrace, and the sin would be upon his head. So, given the choice of ruining two lives, Gopal chose to ruin Lena's.

'Perhaps,' Raj wrote us savagely, 'the young intellectual feels that her degree will keep her warm at night.'

With this, the Kirits drew even closer together. To Sheela, whose condition had been deteriorating, Lena's misfortune was the last straw. She grew steadily weaker, and died of a haemorrhage towards the end of the year. The house was quiet now; there was no sound of laughter, no sound of the boys running lightly down the stairs. Raj gave up all idea of marriage. As long as he was alive, he said quietly and without dramatics, he would have to look after his sisters – they might be financially independent and academically qualified, but they were women and they needed protection. Jairaj, too, continuing on his usual carefree course, remained a bachelor. Lena and Meena taught, and came home straight from work again, not because they feared scandal now but because the college held nothing to interest them particularly. Lena served on committees, more from a resigned sense of duty than anything else. And Meena had stopped entertaining long ago. They grew fat and rather apathetic, with pasty complexions and an addiction to heavy perfume and florid printed chiffons. Nina went to Hyderabad to work in a hospital, married a wastrel much younger than herself, and spent the rest of her youth and health and sanity supporting him.

We did not see the Kirits for many years. Our own lives were catching up with us; we had not time to visit the south. My sister settled in Bombay, and when I won a scholarship to study abroad, she thought it apropos to remind me about them.

'It doesn't pay being a deviant here,' she said wryly. 'Example, the Kirits.'

'Especially when you don't *want* to be one,' I agreed. 'Example, the Kirits.'

And we spoke of the mother and the girls' tutored horror of being 'different,' and of how different they had eventually become from most of their contemporaries.

When my father went south for a conference, he called on them, and came away with an impression of such intense, even suffocating closeness that, he said, the very house had seemed airless. Jairaj was in bed; his injured leg had started to give him serious trouble and made him a querulous invalid. The sisters took turns nursing him. Lena had been offered a fellowship in a European university, but she declined it – Jairaj had to be looked after, and besides, Meena would miss her, Meena liked feminine company in the house. A few months earlier, an elderly widower had timidly approached the empty-eyed but still beautiful Meena with a proposal of marriage, only to be met with an indifferent refusal. Something had broken in her, she said; she couldn't rouse herself to care for a stranger again. Besides, Jairaj needed nursing and Lena would be lonely without her. Raj watched over them all, getting thin and wizened, his laughter and loquacity dwindling with the years.

'They're trying to *preserve* each other,' my sister summed up, in a muffled voice, to acknowledge partial truth. 'They *have* to, they've no choice. And yet you can't do that. Human beings aren't jam.'

It was last year that I made my own visit to Madras, with my mother. When I saw Lena and Raj, I remembered what my sister had said. The Kirits had sacrificed their individual selves for the family until there was no family left. No one else left. Meena and Jairaj had died, and Nina, once a capable doctor, now shut herself up in a room at the back of the house; her years with the wastrel had proved too much for her. Raj called it a nervous breakdown, and Lena could not bear to think of her sister in a sanatorium. 'They've offered me that fellowship again,' Lena mentioned in passing, 'and of course I've refused once more. I'm needed at home.'

They stood at the front door, waving goodbye when we left. Walking down the drive, I tried to tie up all that had happened with the inexplicable quietness in Lena's eyes. 'Look out!' my mother cried suddenly, jolting me out of my thoughts. I had almost stumbled against one of the betel sellers, who was squatting by the hedge, preparing to pitch a tent there for the night. He had done it for years now, he said. The people in the big house raised no objection. And he smiled a little and looked at the house, its paint peeling and its railings drunkenly askew, old and dilapidated behind the tamarind trees.

Pilgrimage

The irony of hiding anything, especially a part of your own life, is that in the act of picking it up and secreting it you are forced to look at what lies between your hands. Invariably, the first one he saw there was Periyamma.

Whenever any fact in this world or doubt about the next plagued the old lady, she would pack her belongings in a disreputable bundle and announce that she was going on a pilgrimage to the Himalayas; they need never see her again. There would be a moment's silence, general and resigned, then everyone in the house set about placating her.

She had been at it for years – since before Independence, before the Second World War; perhaps, for all Eknath knew, even before he himself was born, when the whole clan, with his father at its head, had moved to the rambling terraced house on what then had been the outskirts of Madras. With the deadly insight of kinship, he could visualize how at the very outset Periyamma (she must have been elderly even then) sniffed out the most unsuitable places in which to put down her roots and nourish her grudges.

There she sat, right through his boyhood, her mat always spread out in the dingiest corner or the draughtiest passageway, coughing reproachfully as anyone passed by. Should the cough go unnoticed, she muttered, 'Who cares about a useless old relative like me? Discarded, that's what I am. Thrown away like a pile of soiled clothes. Left to catch pneumonia in this wind and damp. Best to die, no burden to anyone then. Yes. Best to die –' Until you yourself were halted dead in your tracks and forced to turn remorsefully around, begging her to take back her inauspicious words.

'*Ayyo*, Periyamma! Don't say such things. Please come inside, don't sit there in the draught.'

Mollified then, glancing at the inner room where another bed was being made for her, she would heave a martyred sigh. 'Let me be.

It's all right.'

He should indeed have let her be, never ventured anywhere near those piled bedclothes, the wheedling voice; but these sessions induced bursts of garrulity in her which were hard to evade.

'Come here, Eknath. Tell me what happened in school today.'

'No time to talk, Periyamma. Got to run. Games practice.'

'Oho! Since when?'

Lagging on the doorstep at that moment, he was torn between two importances – the sunlit patch of playground where his friends had gathered, and this gratifyingly ignorant audience of one, waiting to be enlightened. Briefly, like a big shot in the films, he threw out the information at her from the corner of his mouth. 'Inter-school sports. Games captain has flu. I have to take over.'

'Will you win a hundred prizes for your school, my boy?'

'Hundred? Periyamma, what do you know about these things? If I'm lucky I might manage the hurdles and the hundred-yard dash, but the boys think I'll also be able to captain the cricket team.'

That was when she started it, leaning back quite serenely against the wall. 'Oh, you'll do anything anyone expects of you, my boy.'

He was already halfway around the door, but he heard her. Sleepy old sorceress, how could she possibly know what went on in school? The new drawing master – a long-haired dreamer from Shantiniketan who slithered in and out of classes on a continuous wave of dedication – had decreed that Eknath was his one pupil destined for greatness. Inexorably, he guided Eknath toward a whole new language of shape and colour, line and form. Obligingly, Eknath learned to converse in it. Every other subject taught in school dwindled to so much pedestrian clutter. At the end of the month, his father descended from his Olympian study upstairs to thunder over the report card, calling on all their learned ancestors to bear witness to such ignominy.

Then Periyamma said it again, confident as ever. 'He expects you to get a first class in your Matric, my boy. With distinction, mind. Of course you'll get it.'

Eknath did – how could he not? – and the best college in the university opened its fusty, hospital doors to his so-called brilliance.

Friends and relatives preened inordinately over his burgeoning reputation. 'As the son of such a famous social reformer,' they said next, 'he is bound to join the struggle for Independence.'

So he went to a demonstration outside the Ripon Buildings and got hit on the head and was laid up for six weeks.

74

One day, exhausted by the extra work this entailed, his usually gentle young stepmother was driven to fret: 'Invalid children can take the life out of you!' After which he did nothing less. He moaned and complained, lost his appetite, grumbled to be let out of bed, and generally regressed from college youth to stepchild in an instant, until some gossipy neighbours arrived to chat with one of the aunts in the next room.

'Poor thing,' he could hear them sympathizing in the fraught undertones that make you listen in spite of yourself. 'So young and pretty and tied to a man more than twice her age. All this talk of abolishing the caste system and look at the misery it breeds in your own home.' And then, after a significant pause: 'Good thing there are no young men at loose in this neighbourhood.'

What did they mean, no young men, what about *him*? Who the hell were they talking about anyway? Afterwards, Eknath could only conclude that he must have been appallingly naïve – and continued so until the next time his stepmother entered the room, first peeping warily in to gauge his mood. Out of the blue he was wrung speechless with pity. Blind, he'd been. Blind and deaf and callous beyond belief; but habit dies hard. When he finally found his voice it must have sounded as surly as ever. 'Come in, I'm awake.'

He could no longer remember the precise moment at which she had entered his life. there must have been the usual reckoning audience of relatives on the sidelines, waiting and watching to pounce on the first signs of rancour he would exhibit. But for once he had refused to live either up or down to their expectations.

Perhaps he had been too young. Or perhaps it was just that he retained no vivid enough memory of his own mother, against which to deprecate her successor. For too long his mother had been enshrined in family annals as a legend and a scapegoat in one (legend because of her spectacular beauty, scapegoat because of her half-Bengali blood) presumably accounting for what they called her 'emotionalism' which in turn, they claimed, had been handed down to her only son to account for his wayward streak. It was a theory as convenient as the doctrine of *karma* itself: retribution for these ingrained irrationalities would surely come in time as a matter of course and logic. Meanwhile, to have the cause named was to have his guilt cushioned. For too long now, therefore, Eknath had recognized his mother only by the look his elders exchanged after each of his misdemeanours, big or little: 'Takes after *her*, you know.'

His stepmother too came of different blood, being a Reddi from Hyderabad. But in her this very difference in itself became a means of obeying her husband's dictates – by the single act of marrying him, she had automatically broken down the barriers of caste, thus absorbing his ideals and making them her own. Complaisance, that was her way. An unobtrusive merging into the household. She was far too young and malleable to be the stuff of legend.

Looking at her now, Eknath couldn't imagine who in the world had created all those vacuous misconceptions about college boys being most attracted to college girls, with their tossing heads, their saris worn in the slim modern fashion, their many vociferous claims and coquetries. In spite of the loud harangues against the caste system blazoning forth day and night from their house, his young stepmother, for having married into a Brahman family, was swathed in orthodox nine-yard saris, decked to extinction in traditional gold and diamond jewelry, unable to make the slightest movement without betraying burdens of her role: from the jingling bunch of household keys at her waist to the weighted rustle of her clothes to the clinking of bangles on her delicate wrist, now loaded down with books she had brought him to read.

Her fingers brushed his as she handed them over. He almost jumped. She never noticed, merely sensing some new lenience in the atmosphere, perhaps, for she volunteered seriously: 'Your friend Iyer chose them from the University Library. He said they were just what you'd want, nice and nihi – nihilistic.' She stumbled over the unaccustomed word, charming as a child.

Nihilism. Of course, that was the answer. A personal nihilism. How else to combat the agony and guilt, endure the thought of her climbing those steps to their bedroom on her tired little feet, duty to the household followed by duty to the husband, that booming tub-thumping moralist hiding his lechery behind steel-rimmed glasses and a ton of platitudes? Filial piety was so much nonsense; paternity the blight of man; infatuation to incest a step as short or long as any other in life. Or might have been, if she weren't hedged about with innocence, so opaque, almost dense perhaps? Blasphemous thought. No, his goddess only grew more deliciously mysterious by the hour, curtaining off the recesses of her mind to a callow stepson out of sheer reticence and grace.

'What was it like where you lived in Hyderabad?' he asked her next noon when she brought in his lunch.

Her eyes roamed over the platter, enumerating each culled item

76

under her breath: 'Rice, pickles, *avial, sambar* . . .' In the patched and streaky light of the room, blurred by croton leaves outside the window, her face was the only clarity, its pure, beautiful lines undisturbed by either thought or event.

'I said, what was it like where you lived in Hyderabad?'

'Oh, nice. Eat the vegetables, they are good for you!'

'Don't boss me. Where was your house? By a river, on the plain, in the hills, or what?'

'On a hill.'

'What did you see when you looked out of the window?'

Vaguely she brushed a damp tendril of hair from her temple.

'Trees.'

'What else?'

'Bushes.'

'What else?'

'Rocks.'

'No people?'

'There were no roads there, it was quite lonely.'

'Nobody at all, then?'

'Sometimes the Banjara tribespeople used it as a shortcut to the construction site where they worked.

'Magnificent!' He forgot all his leftist sympathies in a burst of sentimentality. 'How colourful they must have looked, coming across the hill!'

'Yes,' she said flatly.

'Didn't you want to change places with them, take on their wandering ways?'

Slowly, the great dark eyes lifted from the food to stare at him, nonplussed. 'Why should I? They have their lives, I have mine.'

Resumption of college routine saved his ardour from being doused on the spot. He stoked it carefully, carrying her exquisite image in his mind all day long: no cliché too resounding to describe her tragedy, his slender sacrificial lamb slaughtered at the altar of social reform. . . . Soon Iyer and the other fellows took to exchanging glances, then nudging him, then guffawing: 'Lovesick, ah? Who's the girl, new neighbour, ah?'

ii

The neighbours themselves, those same gossipy ladies, came up with a more plausible conjecture. Returning late from class one evening, he was too preoccupied at first to notice them on the main thoroughfare that led to his street. The sidestreet was quiet but the main road deafening as usual that evening with the crowds and clamour of traffic – a familiar, dust-thickened layer of noise above which rose the two unmistakably fraught voices behind him.

'Hit on the head, wasn't he? May have unhinged him a bit. Made him turn odd – you know, eccentric.'

No doubt confirming their suspicions, Eknath digested that, standing immobile at the turnoff where his street joined the main road. This is where ghosts supposedly reside, phantom centre of the parting of ways, propitiated by small offerings: a few marigold petals, some *kumkum*, a twisted yellow piece of turmeric laid in the dust. Today the offerings were shared by a milestone at the corner, its prosaic legend, '3 furlongs', daubed with a broad vermilion streak – due obeisance paid to some unknown god of distances, perhaps, or to the spirit of the neem tree spreading its branches above. Watching the nervous delicacy of the leaves fretted against the sky, Eknath savoured his crossroads to the full. So symbolic, so easy at this stage to rise to the appellation: pass his final exams next month and then take off, a master's degree behind him and unlimited eccentricities ahead. The departure would be garlanded with many regretful tongue-clickings: 'Could have had a brilliant career . . . too erratic . . .' No one knowing why he fled, carrying the image of his unattainable love with him.

His unattainable love was at that moment returning from the temple. When she saw him she cried out at once: 'What are you doing, standing in the middle of the road? You'll get run over.'

If he had to be flattened by anything, better by a bus than by bathos. Why couldn't their actual conversations ever measure up to his imagined ones? Oneiric mistress, lovely dark denizen of his dreams, for whom he would have taken willing leaps into chaos, plunged into any extent of absurdity or worship – now that she was actually hurrying along beside him, he could not even bring himself to point out the milestone to her, merely watch the softness of her hair vying with the softness of her mouth, and wonder desperately what she was thinking about. The evening's menu, most likely.

'I'm leaving.' Abruptly the words were torn out of him.

(Where? Where will you go? Oh, don't leave me –) 'For the holidays, you mean? Good idea. You'll need some rest after working so hard for the exams. Hurry up, now. There's *rasam* for dinner tonight.'

78

Their doorway loomed up in the dusk. 'I mean away. I'll go away and never return.'

(Why, why? What have I done, my dearest?) 'Don't joke.' Even her reproofs were placid. 'You're too old for such things. Now go in and wash up or you'll be late for dinner.'

Stomping in, he was halted by the familiar skinny arm held out above the bedclothes. 'Stop,' Periyamma said peremptorily. 'I heard you. You are quite right. The sooner you leave, the better.'

They were staring at each other, suddenly enemies: Eknath a craven one, for she frightened him more than his own emotions had, simply by taking them seriously.

'Did you hear me?' Not a trace of the usual muttering senility in her imperious tone. How the devil had she found him out? Had he carried his clichés to an inexcusable extreme and talked in his sleep?

Her fierce whisper answered him. 'Can't keep your eyes off her, can you?' followed by the verdict again delivered loudly as a judge. 'Yes. The sooner you leave the better.'

'How can you say such a thing?' Delicate, shocked, his stepmother had flown out into the corridor, the shadows of her upraised arms stretching gracefully out like wings behind her on the wall. Trying to defend him, his unbearable love. If her beauty didn't kill him, her stupidity would.

'Eknath knows how,' the old one stated, assuming one of her most serenely matriarchal poses against the wall. 'I expect he will leave.'

Eknath did.

The social reformer (by some numbing and merciful process of mental amputation, he ceased to be a parent from that night) was away reforming in the capital, obviating a thunderously wrathful scene. The aunts and cousins were out; Periyamma snoozed, relapsing into murmuring somnolence as soon as her lucidity had served its purpose. Even the neighbours had gone off somewhere, their house humped dark and silent against the night sky.

She intercepted him, soft and urgent, standing just beside his shoulder in the dimness of the garden, to plead with him for the last time. 'Why are you doing this foolish thing? There is such a thing as carrying a joke too far.'

There was such a thing as carrying innocence too far. Before he knew it his arms were around her. Crushed, breathless, she did not even struggle: stood utterly passive in his embrace until she seemed to be a part of him, in a stillness so total, so deep, that it had become sexless. Angrily he wanted to move against her, fling her to the damp garden earth; but his will evaporated – in the face of that stillness, he could not stir. How long they stayed together he did not know.

Obviously not too long. Perhaps as long as it took her mind to transmute his passion into an impulsive but basically filial gesture. Or to remember that the neighbours might be home any minute. Or recall some item to be put away in the kitchen. Before she could turn restive against any of these reminders he had gone.

Away from her, the gate swinging shut behind him; the street lamp foggy, as if made part of his own exhalation; the pavement not a separate substance but an extension of his own homeless foot. This was how men turned into statues, or died, or grew. There would be other women. There were. None able to give him as much, mindlessly and absolutely, as that after all chaste embrace in the dark.

iii

Even the clichés had deserted him. No wry ironic stance to salve his pride, no parodies to save his face.

Eknath tramped the streets of Madras all night. Bazaars and quiet residential areas. Lonely dawn-lit roads where farmers trundled in their produce for the morning market and milkmen cycled past, clattering their tin cans. A cycle repairman turned the corner and came towards the tree where Eknath had finally stopped to rest.

Perhaps he would speak, make the world sane again with a single unconscious epigram. He merely burped, scratched his head, and wound his turban tighter. Then, reaching up, he slung a bicycle tyre on the branch to advertise his trade, sat down under it and began to spread out his implements one by one on a sheet of old newspaper. Eknath watched, the man spread. No comment. In a repairman's eyes, every creature must be an appendage to his machine; without such a *raison d'être* Eknath simply did not exist. It was very restful not to exist.

'Do you want something?' the man asked at last. 'Or shall I call the police?'

Before the next farmer had trundled past, they were matching truculence for truculence. 'All right, you call the police, and I'll charge you for making false allegations.'

The repairman looked him up and down, disgusted. 'You are educated.'

'I am,' Eknath admitted, disgusted in his turn. 'For all the good it has done me.'

His companion split the morning with a deafening guffaw and hostilities lightened. 'What are you doing this time of the morning, drunk?'

'Ran away from home.'

'Oh.' Again his eyes swept Eknath up and down, pausing at the pockets to weigh their contents.

'Penniless,' Eknath qualified, not quite accurately.

The man returned to his tools and rearranged the last row. 'What was the trouble, failed in your exams'?' The faint sneer crept back into his tone. 'That's what these students do if they fail. Run away or hang themselves or drink poison. If I could read and write, I wouldn't worry about exams; right off I'd start a garage with two mechanics working under me, and do all my own accounts. That's the main thing. Never hand over money matters to anybody else. Look at what happened to my brother-in-law. . . .' While he held forth on his brother-in-law, Eknath squatted down next to him and must have dozed off a little, exhausted by all his walking, for he woke to hear the repairman end triumphantly: 'And so he left his job and joined the Congress Party.'

Of course! That was the answer. All rebellious young men these days were expected to enlist in the local branch of the Congress Party. What further incentive did he need? Not in Madras, however. That was too close to home. Thanking his unwitting benefactor, Eknath tottered off to get a cup of coffee and a third-class ticket to Madanapalle.

Here a self-styled Publications Division brought out pamphlets, circulars, and even a fortnightly paper called *The Charkha* (with its titular spinning wheel adorning the masthead), distributed over certain sections of the South. There was practically no pay involved – nobody, especially in these fly-by-night organizations, could afford much. Nevertheless he got living quarters with the subeditor, and an elderly widow in the neighbourhood took charge of their ration cards and fed them both. In some ways this impromptu makeshift quality of their lives, drawing the small staff still closer together, became more important to Eknath than their combined zeal for the cause. He and his roommate did most of the desk work, from writing and editing to planning the layout and correcting proofs.

One day, after a public meeting, when they were sitting around the big dealwood table that functioned as an 'office', waiting for the galleys to roll off the ancient press, Eknath found himself beginning to doodle on a scrap of paper. Wartime paper: thick and brown, smudging every stroke like a blotter. But under his fingers the lines inexplicably curved and stretched and came together, reassembling the meeting of the day before: crowds, volunteer workers, the main speaker at the event standing pompous and potbellied on the dais. It was the first time he'd held a drawing pencil in his hand since leaving home, mainly because anything he drew turned into his stepmother – the delicate curve of her cheek, the gentle tilt of head and wrist, the enormous unforgettable eyes. . . . Here at last had he staved off the peril then?

The relief he felt, staring at it, was nothing to the astonished delight of the editor when he reached across to borrow a file folder, saw the drawing, and began to laugh. 'You did that? Wonderful! Look at this fellow's eye on the pretty volunteer. And that boy pulling his sister's plaits. And *this* character –' jabbing Eknath's portrait of the main speaker – 'you don't have to put a label on him, he's a bloody politician right there. You don't miss much, man. Damn it, with a talent like this I'd expect you to be a cartoonist.'

Eknath had no choice but to turn into one. After one of their haphazard staff meetings, they decided to run a box on the front page, simple entitled 'Today' and bearing no further captions. In it he drew anything that struck him: from his mascot, the cycle-repairman, to Periyamma on her mat, to street scenes, to political rallies, and finally to the granite visage of the police sergeant who came to confiscate what he called 'subversive material' from the dealwood desk and found that *The Charkha* had folded, his quarry fled. (Eknath caught his profile from a neighbour's window.)

iv

The last sketch, of course, never appeared. But he took it with him as a momento on a hike up the hill of Horsleykonda, where he spent half his meagre salary paying for room and board at the Travellers' Rest House: a solitary, capacious building crowning the thickly-wooded summit. His days there were heady with the lightness of knowing he had nothing more to lose – of approximating, in lay terms, what Kalidasa must have meant when he spoke of owning the whole world upon disowning yourself.. . . He might even have begun a portrait of his stepmother; instead he drew trees.

There was little else on this side of the hill, except for the squat stone pillars of the Rest House festooned with graceful drooping wisteria; a half-ruined shack at the other end of the garden where two missionary ladies were reputed to have fought off a bear during the intrepid 1800s; and an outcropping of rock some way beyond the house. Here Eknath spent a whole frustrating day trying to sketch a tree he couldn't identify. All he knew was that it ascended in clouds of burnished copper to the sky, and that he could no longer draw straight: beneath his pen it was a caricature of a tree. That wry ironic stance cultivated so carefully during his college days had become a blight at his fingertips, impossible to shed. He was so dismayed, so absorbed in despairing the fact and deploring his tree, that he paid no attention to the footsteps coming up the rocks. Finally a voice said in impeccable Oxonian accents: 'I say, that's rather splendid, you know.'

Mr Daruwalla. It was all there at first sight: the unmistakable brand of name and money and consequence. A beaky, fair-skinned Parsi face topped the incongruous tennis flannels in which he must have roasted, as he stood there claiming with aplomb to have recognized Eknath as *The Charkha* artist from his very first glimpse of the drawing. More likely his identity had been revealed by the rheumy old cook attached to the Rest House, when he shambled in to ask what the *sahib* wanted for dinner. But you can't quibble when people offer you jobs, partiuclarly people like Mr Daruwalla who was the spirit and everything else behind that most outspoken of Bombay's daily newspapers, *The Sentinel*.

In some ways, that afternoon encounter was even more improbable than developing a passion for your stepmother. The latter was at least secret and therefore inviolate, his own for the very fact that it was taboo; but this sort of thing, being more or less public property, seemed like one more subject for one more cartoon. It was years before he could admit the connection between his private and professional selves, else he might have been brazen enough to say on that very first evening: 'Take warning. Perhaps I am a cartoonist only because I can't stop laughing at myself or at my feelings – it may not be talent at all, just this grimace that extends to the rest of the world. Do you realize that?'

But that was none of Mr Daruwalla's business. His business was *The Sentinel* and why he considered Eknath right for the paper.

After dinner he held forth on the subject.

'What you do isn't really satire, you know,' Mr Daruwalla said, waving his pipe stem about. 'I'd call it an utterly telling illustration. You are a physical witness to life in our country. That's all. But that *is* all, it's everything. This is why you never need words. You don't call a man a profiteer, it's the way you draw his paunch. Or when the Viceroy makes fatuous comments about how every man, woman, and child must contribute to the War Effort – what do you do? You show us your grandmother. Or whoever that old lady of yours is. Comment enough. Who needs more?'

As their association lengthened over the years, his definitions changed to fit the times. 'Viceroy' was replaced by 'Governor-General' and then 'President'. 'The War Effort' became 'famine relief' or 'flood control' or 'the language issue' or whatever national emergency preoccupied him at the moment. He also took to making statements with the adept air of a connoisseur: 'You have a fine sense of the ridiculous, Eknath, but your forte isn't wit so much as accuracy – the ability to show us the truth, the idiocy at the heart of things.'

He fancied himself quite an orator, did Mr Daruwalla; yet Eknath had much to thank him for ever since that first evening at the Horsleykonda Rest House when they dined together as darkness settled over the forest outside and Mr Daruwalla was so grandiloquently kind and Eknath wondered where it would all lead.

v

Yes, it had led to fame of a sort. He was no longer declared a unique talent now that he was part of the establishment and presumed to need neither prodding nor praise. Besides, Mr Daruwalla had already produced the coping stone of all his rhetoric: 'You will be one of the voices of our paper. I expect you to work wonders.' That bloody phrase again. Dehumanizing to be so ridden by formula, but there it was. Sales had mounted steadily until *The Sentinel* eased itself into place as one of the three top dailies in the country.

In no time at all his position on the paper had acquired a solid air of permanence. He rented a flat within walking distance of the office and scanned the personal columns of several newspapers. For the first few years his stepmother had sent in regular appeals. 'Come back,' they said typically. 'All is forgiven.' What was there to forgive and who, in any case, was supposed to do the forgiving? It was so loving, so obtuse, that he dared not trust himself to reply.

Then on a windy monsoon morning almost ten years after he had left home, *The Sentinel*, like all other papers, ran front-page news of his father's death. By now, after the usual predictions of doom and declarations that sons of famous men are inevitable failures, word must have spread regarding Eknath's whereabouts – how could it not, in a country where the fastest news from the Rg Veda downward has always travelled by word of mouth? God knows he had tried to conceal his identity. Only a section of his name appeared at the bottom of the cartoons. 'Nath', he signed himself, with a huge and flamboyant 'N' waving its arms like a windmill and the rest tailing off into an illegible squiggle.

But now the time had come to make amends. He spent three sleepless nights, dithering, until another aspect of the matter struck him. Maybe she needed help. Maybe his father's relatives were scrounging off the childless widow, trying to do her out of her inheritance –

Eknath did not wait for a train. He wired home and caught the earliest available flight to Meenambakam Airport, using every fraction of energy to still the tumult of mixed motives and emotions that had begun to hound him again after having stayed so safely buried these ten long, barren years.

Predictably, the house was full of relatives, relishing the situation to its utmost, all agog with a ghoulish curiosity that they tried to tone down with many displays of conscious rectitude. Here was an erring son (it is always the son who errs) returning to make peace with his dead father. The wife didn't count. She mourned alone in the room upstairs. Yet when they crowded Eknath up the staircase, he now had enough distance and authority to dispatch them down again without ceremony.

For a terrible moment at the door he was afraid her head might be shaven, demeaned into widowhood; but this was still the house of a social reformer. She wore white and no wifely dot between her brows; the hair lying softly on the nape of her neck remained as dark as ever and the forehead, bereft and smooth, was still as beautiful as a young girl's. How old could she be now? Late thirties? They stared at each other across the room. He had imagined she would burst into tears and was already steeling himself in readiness against what this would do to his self-control. However she made no sound at all, sitting thin and dry-eyed at the window. 'She nursed her husband day and night,' one of the aunts had said downstairs. Was this the reason for her silence then, the endless fatigue in the droop of her shoulders?

'You didn't come when he died,' she said finally.

'No.'

'You come now.'

'Yes.'

'Why?'

'To make sure you are treated well.' The faintest smile curved the corners of her mouth, making a Buddhist sculpture of her face. 'To make sure those vultures downstairs don't cheat you out of anything,' Eknath said angrily.

'Hush, it's all right. I don't want any money.'

'All very well to say that.'

'I mean it.'

'With whom will you stay now?'

'Alone,' she said; and when he looked incredulous: 'I want to go to an *ashram*,' naming a famous hermitage whose presiding saint had recently passed away . . . 'attained *samadhi*,' as the faithful said.

'But the Rishi is no longer there.'

'Don't you think I know that?'

Against the bitterness in her voice he thought equally bitterly: 'Yes, like the rest of them. Religion will be her palliative. That's worse than an opiate because less blind.' Aloud he said gently: 'As you wish. I will escort you there myself.'

They did not speak to each other at all in the few days that followed, except for conversations confined to practicality: the clearing of legal formalities, the transfer of the family home to his oldest cousin. In forfeiting his own right to it, Eknath had forfeited other things as well, like his presence at Periyamma's death. 'She went quietly,' the cousin said. 'No cries, no noise. At night she was there; in the morning, not.' That was all he could feel now: her absence. Bare spots on the wall where her head had rested, on the floor where her mat had been. Nothing else, except perhaps a sense of fitting conclusions. Having delivered Eknath up to what was expected of him, she had accomplished her peripheral *dharma* of getting him out of the house, and then gone herself. Now the vestiges of her action were going too.

A delegation of relatives gathered for a send-off at the railway station, as if to underline their approval of the proceedings: she was

behaving as a grieving, world-weary widow should; he had at last
come to his filial senses. They travelled by first-class coupé on the
narrow meter-gauge lines of the South. At first the sadly decorous
farewells had taken up most of the room in the carriage, then the
dispersal of luggage – bundles on racks, boxes under seats.

Now his coat swung to and fro on its hook by the door; her
delicate profile was etched against the flying landscape as she stared
steadily out of the window, not speaking at all. Silence filled the
compartment, grew louder than the clatter of wheels. She had
changed after all. Once she might have sought to fill the quiet with
chit-chat, meaningless questions about his well-being, his job.
Mouthing all the parrot politenesses for which our women are
trained from their birth, Eknath thought: learn to yield, learn to
placate. . . . Without saying a word, she was telling him what it was
like to be a woman.

vi

They had set out early in the evening. Now a smothered moody
sunset hovered raggedly above the trees, dipping its sheen into
ponds and waterways, and tinting the earth a subtle red outside.
Out of courtesy to her silence he took a book from his bag – nice
and nihilistic, he might have said years ago; but soon it had grown
too dark to read. Overhead the sky dimmed, windows began to
glimmer in houses and huts. The smoke from countless dung fires
stretched like mist across the fields and over the mud-walled villages
they passed, invading the train windows with its acrid evening smell.

When at last she spoke, it was to say gently: 'That is not the kind
of book to read in a dark train, is it?'

Open on his lap was a rather rabid treatise of political philosophy.
'How do you know?'

'I read to him, these last few years, when his eyesight failed.'

Eknath digested the picture: they must have achieved some
mental companionship as well then, in the months of his illness and
physical dependency on her.

'Why do you never speak of him?' she pursued, still gentle,
inexorable. 'Why would you never face him, not even to say
good-bye when you left? It hurt him very much.'

Should he tell her the truth, admit: 'If I confronted him as my
father, I had to accept you as his wife. Irredeemably, inaccessibly
his wife.' But he only said in the old surly way: 'He had no time for

me, why should I have time for him?'

'When he was younger he was busy. Most fathers are, that is not so unusual, is it? What is strange is that a son should behave to his father as you did to him.'

'That is only in a tradition-choked country like ours. In some cultures, in the West, for instance, it is accepted as part of the pattern of life for children to rebel against their parents.'

'What has *that* got to do with us?'

Eknath did not reply. Even more gently, she said: 'Forgive me, I had to speak to you about this.'

'And express your displeasure?'

'I wish I could have done something to make you understand one another better.' In the half-dark he caught the arrested helplessness of her voice and gesture. 'It was my duty as your –'

'You're not my mother,' Eknath said roughly. At which, imagining she had affronted the memory of his own mother, she apologized again, irritating him so much that he burst out: 'You are nearer my age than his. It was not right, it was not proper.'

'What right have you to pass judgment on that?'

'As much right as you have to pass judgment on my behaviour. What can you know –'

'What can *you* know?' With the sudden overwhelming authority of anger she wrested the words from him, all the old placating gentleness gone. 'You live in your world of ideas, what can you know of hunger and poverty and the pain of being a woman? My father was ill. There was no money for either medicine or food.'

'You mean my father bought you?'

In the silence he heard her catch her breath. 'Don't you see,' she said. 'Better your father than some evil old landlord or moneylender.'

Life sometimes leaves you no time to ingest what it has made you swallow. Always, so far, he had consigned this sort of situation to the drivel of third-rate films. . . . The wheels rattled slower; his stepmother remarked, a little shakily but otherwise in her usual voice, 'It looks as if we're coming to a station. Better turn on the lights or they'll think this is an empty compartment and try to get in.'

He muttered some reassurance about standing guard at the door and stumbled out. It was a small wayside stop. The sliding blur of the platform resolved itself into a mad scramble as half-a-dozen passengers tried to push their way in through the nearest door and were told to enter a carriage further down. A solitary vendor sold tea in earthen cups, his voice floating further and fainter away as the bell clanged and the train moved on again into the night.

Returning to the compartment he managed to ask, casual and quotidian: 'Are you hungry, would you like to eat?'

She first asked, 'Are you?' and when he said no, elected obediently to wait. Neither made a move to switch on the light. In the dark it was easier to apologize, to say: 'I have much to ask your pardon for.'

'And his.' Was there an overtone in her voice, was she at last beginning to see? 'He was kind,' she said. 'It was not a buying. He paid for my education, he helped my father, he wanted no dowry. My parents were very grateful.'

'And you?'

'Yes. Now I am grateful.'

'But *then*?'

No answer.

'Then you were so young.'

Still no answer.

He dared further. 'And so beautiful.' And so stupid only because you couldn't afford to think?

This time he thought her silence would not be proof against his will. That perpetual demon on his back was goading him to ask: 'If he really wanted to save you from your circumstances, why didn't he arrange your marriage to someone nearer your own age? To me?'

Before he could utter any of it, she remarked matter-of-factly, 'It was in my *karma*.'

'*What*?' In the darkness his eyes groped for her face but could see nothing. He couldn't move to turn on the lights, couldn't speak for fear of saying brutally and irrevocably: 'It is in your *karma* to be desired by your stepson then.'

It was no use. The time for confession, the comfort of honesty, was gone. Perhaps if he had stayed on, perhaps if he had played his cards right, perhaps in those days when he had thought she was stupid. . . . His own stupidity really. It was a slim and outrageous chance at best, and by now too much had happened. Somewhere, somehow, facing this tired woman, he had lost his old arrogance; and she had lost her youthful pliancy, learning her way to God knows what stony truth while she tended her sick man. If he touched her with *his* truth now, he would lose her altogether,

89

besides doing her irreparable harm. She might even spend the rest of her days atoning in that hermitage for what was no fault of hers. No, no use at all. She had detached herself far too effectively beyond his ken, and the hell of it was that he still could not stop caring for her – could only perhaps, in the end, hope to face the fact without making a caricature of it.

Yet that night, in an insistent postscript, he dreamed of her. Not an untouchable arm's length away as she lay on her railway berth, but younger and familiarly his; resting her hand on his shoulder as she leaned close to admire the drawings scattered on his desk, laughing until her breath fanned his cheek. When he took her in his arms it was more than a sexual ending to a dream, it was with that wholeness of knowledge possessed by the temple carvings of Konarak and Khajuraho: a saying 'yes' in recognizing how physical, creative, and religious acts can be inextricable parts of the same experience. He woke groggy and unkempt, but he knew why she had need of a hermitage.

vii

Red-tiled roofs clustered between shadowy mango groves; a shining sickle of a river curved hazily away behind into the distant rim of the horizon.

When she saw it she lost her habitual calm and cried out in delight: 'It's beautiful!' The first spontaneous expression of pleasure he had ever heard from her. Himself, Eknath was more enamoured of her reaction to the place than of the place itself, picturesque though it indubitably was, and every bit as peaceful as she wished.

'Welcome, *saar*, welcome!' A bustling, voluble little man shot out of the manager's office, apparently reconciling with enthusiasm his varied roles as entrepreneur, the late saint's brother, and unofficial tourist guide. All the way to her room he regaled them with details about the town, its temple ('early Chola, *saar*'), its climate ('very salubrious, *saar*'), its reservoir being built upriver under the current Five-Year Plan ('the Chief Minister has expressed great interest, *saar*') and the soulful advantages of the hermitage itself ('very good influence on our townspeople, *saar*'). Then another batch of visitors claimed his attention and they were left alone.

Her room was in a long, low-flung building overlooking the water. It boasted a wall cupboard, a table, a chair, and a cot, with a single electric bulb hanging from the ceiling. While she put away her

90

few belongings, Eknath gripped the veranda rails outside and dutifully admired the scenery. Even after the small silken rustle of her movements had ceased behind him, he could not bring himself to turn around and say the final good-bye; there was still that fraction of resentment left. He continued to stand there, learning the river by heart, and her presence continued to heckle him. The impasse was broken by the manager hurrying back on the wings of an afterthought to suggest hospitably: 'Why not stay the night, *saar*? We have rooms available.'

And prolong the agony? Thanks. Eknath shook his head, proferring polite, wholly fictitious pleas of work to be done and appointments to be met. Trained in tact, his stepmother waited until the man was out of earshot. 'Why not do as he says? It has been a long journey, you must be tired.'

Eknath shook his head again.

'Then come sit by the river and rest awhile.'

It was so startlingly unlike her to take the initiative in this fashion that Eknath turned around, and met her eyes as dark and luminous and tender as they had been in his dream. He backed away, momentarily confused. Was this innocence or knowledge? Surely she would be chary of showing her affection if she recognized the quality of his? Or wouldn't she?

No, this was something else again, an impersonal tenderness. She must feel so securely anchored in the simplicity of this place that she could afford to let her loving kindness flow untrammelled. That was all.

He plunged blindly down the veranda steps and toward the river.

Catching up, she said softly: 'Don't worry. You think too much.'

Eknath stopped short in exasperation. 'What do you mean?'

'This.' Her fine-winged brows drew together, suddenly very stern and preoccupied. 'When you do this, it means you are worried or upset. Don't be. Everything is all right now. Look how peaceful it is here.'

Crested wavelets shimmered towards the opposite shore, their ripple the only sound in the sunlit air. Overhead a kite circled, lazily watchful; the shade of the riverbank where they stood was brushed with a cool breath coursing off the water. Eknath bent down to pick up a flat stone and sent it skimming across the ripples, once, twice, thrice.

Unexpectedly she laughed. 'I used to do that as a child.'

He was startled all over again. She had actually volunteered some

91

information about herself without its having to be prised out of her!

'Would you like to try?'

'Oh, no!' Her turn to back away now, hiding her laughter behind her hand, guilty as a truant schoolchild.

'Come on,' he coaxed. 'Just once.'

She glanced hastily around to make sure no one was watching, then took the stone from him – warm fingers scrabbling briefly against his palm – and threw. The stone sailed off in an uncertain arc and descended with a plop, sinking to the bottom.

That made them laugh together, all previous constraint and notions of dignity forgotten. While he skimmed a few stones further and further away, she settled herself on a rock at the river edge, if anything even lovelier and more graceful than she had ever been. Looking at her now, he could see that her earlier tranquility had merely been an unswerving exercise in self-control. Now she was relaxed, open as a flower opens; her beauty all the more complete because it did not withhold her sorrow and denial and loss. He flung himself on the grass at her feet and hunted in his pocket for a cigarette, smoking furiously, unreproved. Her way of touching him, for better or for worse, was to lap him in a peace he was unwilling to accept.

'Will you go back to Bombay now?'

In that instant – an instant made of sun and water and her presence at his side – he made up his mind. 'No. I intend to resign my job.'

'*What*?'

'Yes.'

'But what will you do then? How will you manage?'

'As you do. You have your ways of renouncing the world, I have mine.'

For a moment her anxiety changed to half-laughing disbelief. 'You mean you'll become a wandering mendicant?'

'Perhaps. Though that too might get boring after a while. In which case I'll pick up an odd job or two as I go along.'

'Jobs are not easy to get.'

'Don't you think I know that?'

Mistaking his vehemence, she asked gently: 'Was it very hard for you when you left us ten years ago?'

'What? Oh, that. No, not difficult at all. I got this job within the first six months and have been there ever since. They've been good to me.'

'Then why do you want to leave now?'

'Because I want to be alone, because I want to travel, because I want to paint.'

'*Paint*?' This was the realm of lunacy.

'That is, if I haven't gone too rusty by now, which I may have.'

'But what can you earn with that?' she expostulated. 'How will you live? You won't even touch a *paisa* of your father's property!' Here it was again, beyond doubt. At their closest, they would be most inaccessible to each other.

'Don't worry,' he said in his turn, smiling at her anxious face. 'I have some money saved, I'll be all right. If I find I can't paint, I'll do something else. I can never go back to my cartoons now, that's all.'

She did not press him after that, withdrawing once again into her quiet and leaving him alone. Their interlude was over. He looked at his watch and rose. 'Here is my address. When I give up that flat I'll send you a post office box number, in case you need to reach me for any reason. I have to go now.'

They walked back to the *ashram* together. At her door she stood as if in a niche, still and sculpted white, gravely tilting her head in a gesture of farewell and assent.

viii

Since then he had – 'travelled', he supposed could describe it. Once someone at a chance encounter (one of the many people met on one of the many journeys) had likened his wandering to a *Bharat darshan*: the age-old ideal of a pilgrimage across the length and breadth of the country to be vouchsafed the sight, and thereby the blessing, of your whole holy motherland. Holiness was too doubtful a dimension for the likes of him but he had seen the countryside all right. From the southernmost tip of Cape Comorin, where three seas meet, all the way north to Kashmir for an object and abject lesson on poverty in paradise; then slowly east to the low-lying, thatch-roofed, mud-walled villages of rural Bengal, its ponds choked with incomparable blue of water hyacinths, its air with the stench of jute rising in the ditches; then south-west again to the hamlets strung along the canals of Kerala, whose beguiling, amphibious children slipped smooth as otters from doorstep to water and back again. Mainly, however, he found himself hearkening back to those parts of the South he knew the best – sauntering down country roads; watching the rice fields stretch flat away on

93

either side toward the distant majesty of some temple *gopuram* towering on the horizon; sharing his midday meal with urchins, sharing his midnight watch with Orion spread-eagled above.

Yet when he looked for any reaffirmation, any truth, albeit an outsider's one, since he did not work the soil himself – there was none. Always he had carelessly assumed that what is termed your native heath can be blight or blessing, depending on your apprehension of the moment. To him it was neither. Vastly indifferent, it became a piece of geography alone, finally making no impact because it made no allowances for a corresponding geography of the soul. The land remained; he, walking through it, had to reckon with the changing contours of the self. Like the wandering ascetics whose lives he mimed, he too was being slowly and irreversibly pared away, travelling lighter and lighter over the years. Of the old need and ability to paint, not a trace remained – some competence, yes; the substance, the urgency no.

Now all of Mr Daruwalla's eloquence and grandiloquence no longer wielded power over him. He found he could drop out of circulation as noiselessly as old Periyamma had, nondescript to others, as to himself.

Only once, squashed into a third-class compartment on the southern railway, he surprised his own face in the window pane. It floated like a mirage – ridged, bony profile; mat of greying hair; glasses giving back the raucous glare of station lights – superimposed on a hurrying clutch of humanity with waiting rooms yawning cavernously behind them and a procession of dog-eared posters above, extolling the virtues of everything from Arvind textiles to Ajanta caves. He was so enticed and hypnotized, shifting focus from his own ageing face to the station and back again, that he forgot to read the name of the town when they started to pull out. Then a small obstreperous child, bouncing up and down opposite, called shrilly to its mother: 'Look, the *ashram*!' The train gathered speed, his mirage wavered, and the lights reflected on his glasses became dizzying streaks that suddenly faded into dark. As if in answer or antiphony, a row of lamplit windows shone between the trees.

Dr Salaam

Dr 'Salaam' was what he eventually came to be called by his patients, because they couldn't twist their tongues around his real name, which was Schlamm. 'Salaam,' they would greet him 'salaam, Dr Salaam,' and he would salaam back with equal gravity.

We saw him first when he moved into the Hibinett house, next door. It was called the Hibinett house because a wealthy Swedish match manufacturer of that name had once lived there and startled the entire neighbourhood by singing operatic arias at the top of his voice in the middle of the night. But nobody complained, because, after all, the man had a right to sing in his own house, and since he was far from his country and did not have any family in evidence, it was concluded that he must be lonely and in need of recreation. Foreigners had strange ideas; this was probably one of them.

The Hibinett house was the newest building in the Nungambakam locality of Madras, where we lived, and where most of the other houses were about a hundred years old. The oldest servants in the servants' quarters said that our particular neighbourhood had been inhabited at the turn of the century by Japanese merchants, some of whom had continued to live there until just a few years before the Second World War. These men kept cats, and in the half-dark of an early southern twilight you could still see silent feline shapes skulking along the garden walls or rummaging through the garbage. It wasn't until Dr Schlamm arrived with his enormous marmalade, Toni, that the Japanese cats were routed once and for all, Toni emerged from his battles with a ragged tail and generally moth-eaten fur, but the earlier cats left and Dr Schlamm and his Toni considered themselves well established in their own domain. Every evening, we heard the Doctor, who was both absent-minded and nearsighted, walk up and down the gravelled drive, calling for his cat.

The driveways of the Nungambakam houses were all shadowed

and cool; their gardens stirred with green depths. The garden walls were mellowed to the beautiful dignity of sun-warmed stone, and the tamarind trees that lined the drives had a way of placing a person in his perspective, giving him an inevitable location, with textures of his past and present woven into the shadows they threw around him. Under those trees you could see, for instance, that Dr Schlamm was an Austrian Jewish refugee, about thirty-five, a lonely man; that he had come to India some years ago and taken it to heart – the whole unwieldy, contradictory mass of it – and been embraced as cordially in return. But the sense of being alien had remained, and he was assuaging his loneliness for the first time now, as he told us, by smiling at his neighbours.

Actually, Dr Schlamm had met my father long before he smiled at any of us. In fact, his decision to move into the Hibinett house had stemmed from this meeting, which had occurred soon after his arrival in India during the early years of the war. Characteristically, my father had spoken little of this, so it wasn't until very much later that I heard the incident described by Dr Schlamm himself.

Ten years ago, he said, he had started his practice in Madras by establishing the Schlamm Clinic on Mount Road, where he lived in a poky little room above the office and ate at an Irani restaurant across the street. The practice fared better than he expected, and when the New Year came around, he took two weeks off to go down to a seaside village he had heard about, four hundred miles south and facing the strait between India and Sri Lanka. My father, in government service, happened at that time to be magistrate for the district in which the village lay.

It was a smaller village than any Dr Schlamm had yet seen. There was a cluster of mud huts along the coast (fishermen), near the fields (farmers), and beside the new road (labourers); and one solitary brick house with a bright-red tiled roof. The brick house, staffed by a cook and a caretaker, was called a Travellers' Bungalow, and had been built by the government to accommodate officers touring on duty in the more remote districts. It consisted of two sets of rooms with a veranda all around, where the roof sloped steeply down to meet a row of supporting wooden pillars. Here Dr Schlamm sat in an easy chair, smoking and watching the sea and thinking his thoughts. In the mornings, he swam; in the afternoons he went for a walk along the fields or by the sea, followed by an inevitable column of ragged children with their fingers in their mouths, staring at him because he was probably the first white man they had ever seen – apart from a British official who had once visited the village six years ago, when they were too young to remember anyway.

But it was understood that Dr Schlamm was not an official; neither was he British. He spoke German, and this was during the war, so, though they smiled shyly at him, they kept their distance. Then one day the sleepy old caretaker suddenly came to life and began to sweep the veranda; the cook rushed around with preparations for an elaborate meal – until a dusty jeep came bumping along the village road and a red-coated peon from the magistrate's office hopped out and told them to keep everything as simple as possible because the magistrate-*dorai* disliked fuss.

The magistrate-*dorai* arrived late at night, and turned out to have an unobtrusive chuckle at the back of his voice. When he invited Dr Schlamm to dinner, the Doctor told us he found a man who bore his authority without pretensions, wearing it rather like a dispensable suit – a man who had travelled much and read much and knew his country with the precision and detachment of an ideal Man of Duty lauded by the Bhagavad-Gita. 'It was there in your father that I saw for the first time all the qualities embodied in one man,' he said. 'The combination of a personal and impersonal integrity, the emphasis on a deed for its own sake, the irrevelance of any reward – all of it lightened by a sense of humour. It was fascinating.'

Next day, Father was away on a tour of inspection, and during the drowsy part of the afternoon the hum of an airplane first began. Dr Schlamm was reading, and only registered the fact at the back of his mind. It was a common enough sound in Madras; it did not strike him that this was a remote village, that the sound might be alien here. It died away in the distance and then came back again, faded and reappeared, getting louder and lower – apparently the plane was circling the bungalow. He put down his book and went out to investigate. He was still standing on the veranda, leaning against a wooden pillar and blinking up at the afternoon sky, when he became aware of something else. A crowd was collecting at the gate of the Travellers' Bungalow – a crew of dusty roadworkers and angry-looking farmers. The women and children had been shooed off to one side, where they stood clustered and apprehensive in the scraggly shade of a thorn tree. All of them were talking at the same time, looking from Dr Schlamm to the airplane and then from the plane back to Dr Schlamm again. Meanwhile, the plane itself continued to circle, drowning the chatter of voices each time it came overhead. Dr Schlamm sensed something more than excitement now. The men were gesticulating, pointing to him and drawing closer together. Suddenly uneasy, he called to the caretaker, who was staring up at the sky, openmouthed and speechless. Asked for an explanation, the man only shook his head. Either his English was not equal to the occasion or, more likely, he was unwilling to speak; and Dr Schlamm, at this stage of his stay in India, knew no Tamil. Then there was a sudden concerted movement in the crowd.

'What is it?' the Doctor demanded. 'For God's sake, man, what is it?'

The note of urgency in his voice penetrated at last to the caretaker. He grinned nervously, and jerked his thumb at the plane. 'You bring?' he suggested, and grinned again.

'*No*!' Dr Schlamm said. 'I don't know anything about it. Tell them so! Look.' He turned to the angry, frightened faces at the gate and shook his head, pointing up at the plane and making vehemently negative gestures.

Their expression did not change. They had stopped talking now; the silence had grown ugly. Just then the plane swept down again, lower than it had before, and started to drop leaflets.

He stared in a kind of petrified amazement. The papers floated down, swaying and eddying in the sea breeze and then being carried off to the sands beyond the gate. One of the children ran to pick them up and was arrested by a hoarse shout from his mother – as if in terror of unknown dangers from the sky. With that shout, something broke loose in the crowd. They pushed the gate open and started toward Dr Schlamm with a furious, low-throated roar. 'I thought I was finished,' he said. 'They were going to kill me.' At that moment, like a rattling *deus ex machina*, the jeep came bumping down the road. Before the red-coated peon could hop off, Father was out of the jeep and in among the men. Dr Schlamm had a confused impression of voices and hands, as the crowd was made to halt in its tracks.

'Don't thank me,' Father said afterward, smiling rather dryly. 'It was only the voice of authority they listened to.' He poured the Doctor a stiff drink and explained that the plane had apparently been on a reconnoitring flight, dropping leaflets to assure the people (in English, which not one of them could read) of the harmlessness of its purpose and the need for secrecy.

'But why *me*?' Dr Schlamm demanded, bewildered.

'The villagers knew you'd come from Germany. There were

rumours of a raid. So they put two and two together and made five and a half . . .'

And there, in the red-tiled house by the sea, Father and Dr Schlamm had laughed together and become friends.

But in any case we could not have guessed all this in the beginning, when the Doctor first arrived next door. My father had long since handed over his post to his successor in that southern district; his offices were now in the Madras Secretariat buildings behind the massive walls of Fort St George. He and my mother happened to be away when Dr Schlamm moved in, so we first heard of him when our gardener announced that the man next door seemed rather unusual for a foreigner – quite apart from his habit of calling for his cat up and down the drive. For one thing, he did not have a car; he rode a bicycle. For another, instead of an elaborate staff to run his house, he had a single rascally manservant called Joe, who served as cook, office boy and general factotum. Joe came from a family of second-generation Christian converts, all of whom had died except his mother, a pious and self-effacing woman, who helped her son clean the house, prayed for his soul, and lived in the low-roofed rooms behind the courtyard.

All day, the Hibinett house lay closed and silent. It was built of a particularly dingy shade of bricks; the roof hung low, its eaves beetling everywhere – to the house and the garden and the gravelled drive – until evening, when Dr Schlamm and Joe returned from the clinic. Then Joe set up a terrific banging clatter of pans in the kitchen (as if his mother hadn't done most of the cooking already), and Dr Schlamm went into his study and started to play his records.

He had a magnificent collection, which not only began my personal introduction to Western music but also initiated the neighbourhood's acquaintance with the Doctor himself. Again nobody objected to the volume at which the music was played. My older sister, dreamy and exquisite, and with memories of a European childhood, loved the symphonies that spilled out of his windows and through the trees. But to me these were unknown sounds, and every evening after tea I stood by the hedge between our houses and tried to make sense out of them. One day, I was in my usual place, sucking a surreptitious tamarind (eating too many made you sick), listening to every note and wondering where the next one would fall – too high or too low or not at all – when the hedge parted and a spectacled head thrust itself cautiously through.

'Do you like the music?' Dr Schlamm asked.

Laws of courtesy demanded a positive answer, and laws of truth a negative one; solving the problem, I offered him half my tamarind to suck. He accepted it with a murmured thanks, and clambered through the hedge into our garden and into our lives.

Our household consisted at this time of my parents, whom the Doctor already knew; my older sister, whom he promptly started to fall in love with; me, whose cultural education he took in hand as a matter of course; and a great-aunt, who was alternately charmed and irritated by him but maintained a stony distance (she was fiercely nationalistic and detested Europeans on principle, as part of her fight for freedom). Then there was also Govinda. He was ostensibly a cook but actually more of an old friend, who had come from Kerala to work for my parents long before we were born, bossed us left and right, and had a phobia about cats. He'd disposed of the earlier ones with a summary brandish of his bread knife when they approached too close to the kitchen, but Toni was a different matter. Accepting Dr Schlamm meant making a truce with Toni, so Govinda glowered forbiddingly at the Doctor through the kitchen window, while the Doctor, all oblivious, progressed from neighbour to friend to something much rarer.

It was as if our home reshaped itself subtly around his presence, in a shifting of balance so delicate that neither he nor we were aware of any change. The hedge parted, footsteps sounded across the lawn, and there he was: never a 'visitor', never interrupting the rhythm of the household. His sudden snort of laughter over whatever he was reading became as much a part of the evening as the whirr of the ceiling fan in my father's office room, the rustle of papers on his desk, the soft jingle of household keys as my mother moved in and out of the rooms, the tuneless, thumping harvest songs from the radio programme in Kannada, which was our great-aunt's favourite language, and the crunch of wheels on the gravel as the newsboy delivered the evening paper. When I ran out to read the day's cartoon strip, Dr Schlamm raced me to the doormat and peered over my shoulder. Later, he and my sister did the London *Times* crossword together. And still later, long after we were in bed and the old house had settled down for the night with its customary creaks and groans, he sat out on the lawn with my parents, their voices blending companionably under the stars. There were some nights when they did not talk at all; the only sound then was of the wind lifting the branches of the neem trees – gently, as a woman will lift her hair with her hand to cool the nape of her neck. Often the silence lasted half the night, or so it seemed to us. For my mother – with her intuition so finegrained, so unerring, that only the faintest Japanese brushstroke could begin to define it – always seemed to know when he wanted conversation and when merely the comfort of a human presence.

Others in the neighbourhood were understandably more obtuse. All the same, after that first day when he clambered through the hedge, it was as if Dr Schlamm had moved into the Hibinett house not only physically but with a much deeper tenancy, implying access to our collective loyalty and concern. Our great-aunt, for instance, for all her disapproval, sent up a prayer for the Doctor's safety every time he set out on his bicycle, because she was sure he would end in a ditch. Dr Schlamm's bicycle was an old rattletrap; the brakes never worked; he rode with three fingers of his left hand casually guiding the handlebar, his right hand on his hip and his gaze directed upward to sky or tree-top or telegraph pole, while the bicycle teetered from one side of the road to the other, depending on whether or not he remembered to keep left. 'That man will forget his patients' names next,' our great-aunt scolded.

The trouble was, he did forget them. And Joe was no help, because Joe had a genius for offering his own tactless interpretation of foreign names. 'Oliphants' became Elephants; 'Henri Couchon' turned into Air Cushion; and once a Mrs Willoughby, friend of a friend from a Commonwealth High Commission, departed highly affronted after he had called her Bumblebee, which was unfortunate, because she happened to be a large and buzzing sort of woman. This, though, was not the least of Joe's weaknesses. Every Saturday night, he got roaring drunk and staggered down the road singing lewd songs. Dr Schlamm was never unduly upset, but the auctioneers who had taken the buildings across the road from his saw to it, in a burst of neighbourliness, that Joe was taken safely home each week. Fortunately, Joe yielded to his mother's importunities not to drink on Sundays and spent an abstemious Sabbath nursing his hangover. The auctioneers however, attributed this to the Doctor's good influence and sent him invitations to all their auctions. So one Sunday in every month, Dr Schlamm got the catalogue at their door and wandered dutifully past gate-leg tables and standard lamps and mahogany dressers and out again.

If Joe introduced the Doctor to the auctioneers, Toni was responsible for getting him acquainted with the house on our left.

Toni, for all his prowess in battle, was neurotic about thunder-storms. They drove him under the Doctor's bed, where he crouched, baleful and cowering; and when he did finally emerge, it was to do unpredictable things. Once, he ventured right into our kitchen. We saw a streak of orange, which was Toni, followed by a streak of silver, which was the bread knife gleaming in the sun, followed by a streak of white which was Govinda's dhoti, shoot through the garden and out of the gate. Govinda apologized later, grudgingly, for it had cost him his dignity. But the Doctor proved equally magnanimous. He quite understood Govinda's feelings about cats, he said; why, the cat itself had feelings about thunderstorms, so what could one do? At any rate, one couldn't do anything for the next few days, because Toni disappeared. We looked for him everywhere, but nobody saw so much as a flick of his tail. Then he was discovered hiding in one of the disused lofts in the house to our left.

This belonged to a minor rajah of sorts; he was an obliging little man, tiny and amiable and bald as an egg, and the house to our left was what was discreetly known as his 'establishment'. There was a woman there, buxomly established and with long black hair that she dried in the sunlight up on the roof after her bath. Most of the year, the rajah was away, and the whole place – a huge, humped structure with many rooms – was left to the lady and numerous male servants who spent their time yelling raucously up and down the stairs. One of them found the cat in the loft, but none of them could get near the animal, because of all the hissing and spitting it aimed at them, so finally the lady sent a message asking Dr Schlamm to come and fetch Toni himself.

I watched him over the garden wall, absurdly anxious; that house, for all its noise, had a way of swallowing people up. Dr Schlamm himself seemed embarrassed. He shuffled his shoulders beneath his shirt, scrubbed his feet assiduously on the doormat, and went in. After a while, there was a murmur of voices and a sudden yowl from indignant Toni followed by another murmur. Eventually, the Doctor appeared, a streak of cobweb trailing his cheek, scratches along his hand, bearing Toni in his arms. 'Nice woman, that,' he said to us over his shoulder. 'I told her I'd attend on her if she needed any medical help. You don't suppose the rajah will mind, do you?'

The rajah did not seem to mind. He came and went; the lady stayed on the roof drying her hair. Meanwhile, the Doctor's ideal

102

continued to be my sister – an ideal cherished with a combination of personal need and Petrarchan distance, almost as if her very remoteness was a necessary source of his sustenance: as long as she remained inaccessible, he could remain constant. He probably could have proposed to her at any time, but he never did. The nearest he came to declaring his devotion was murmuring wistfully that this was the kind of girl he'd like to marry; the nearest he came to showing his feelings was by being acutely embarrassed if he happened to be unshaven when she came into the room. How this admiration affected her, I could not tell. She continued exquisite and elusive, away at college or upstairs in her room most of the time, writing poetry or playing on her sitar. My parents, with their usual tolerance, accepted the situation; my mother, with her usual insight, remarked one evening that Dr Schlamm was an anachronism in time and space – no matter where he lived or when he would be out of his context, out of his time. She might have added that when his century caught up with him the disaster would begin, but that we did not know yet.

Or perhaps we did – for with the coming of Medora Hane the neighbourhood arrayed itself on the side of his survival and the fight was on. He told me of the lady one afternoon when I had dragged him off to the Asia Library because I thought I'd discovered a first edition of Burke's *Reflections on the French Revolution* in one of its back rooms. The back room had no door; you jumped over a high window and into another world, filtered with sunlight and dust motes. We sat on the window sill, swinging our legs, our whispers in that place becoming dry as old paper, scrapy as the neem leaves brushing the sandstone ceiling. For when the Doctor discovered it *was* a first edition, he unbent enough to tell me about Medora Hane.

'She works at the U.S. Consulate,' he said. 'One of the staff, in fact. The most beautiful girl I have ever met.'

If that had been all, we might have given our blessing; but she made him sleepless and hollow-eyed, irascible and tormented; what was worse, he lost his appetite and would not eat. There wasn't a moment's joy in the man; he looked almost famine-stricken – and in a country keenly conscious of hunger this would never do. Joe's mother made the first move. She came over, as most of the neighbourhood did in moments of stress, to ask my mother's help. But for once my mother had nothing to suggest. 'There are other needs than the need for rice,' was all she said. So Joe's mother went over to the rajah's establishment, and two days later the lady of the house was ill and needed attention. Dr Schlamm attended her as promised, and before he had time to wonder a little about the symptoms, our gardener's entire family – himself, his wife, his children – had one thing or another wrong with them. They straggled up to his veranda complaining of varied and original illnesses, and Dr Schlamm was too kind to call their bluff. If he did, there was still our chauffeur to be accounted for, and the auctioneer's second cousin, and the Punjabi refugees who were staying with them, and the caretaker from the house behind ours, and lots of runny-nosed two-year-olds, dragged in, protesting, by their mothers, who worked in the houses along the street. Soon there were more patients than he could keep track of. 'Salaam,' they greeted him solemnly every evening. 'Salaam, Dr Salaam.' A makeshift clinic evolved on his veranda; it was always crammed.

All this combined effort paid off. Besides, the glamorous Miss Hane (we saw her once at a concert, and she was every bit as blonde and capricious as expected) had agreed to be escorted to the Saturday-afternoon races at Guindy. Dr Schlamm waited and waited at the appointed hour, but, whether from overpopularity or oversight, she never appeared. After that, the scales fell slowly and obligingly from his eyes, and he went back to eating and sleeping and adoring my sister as usual.

The patients, however, continued to patronize his veranda. Now when we took him to plays, he understood what was being said; when we took him to concerts, he waggled his head in appreciation as enthusiastically as anyone in the audience; he was asked to weddings and was wept on at funerals ('If *you* had treated him, Dr Salaam, he might have lived') – until it seemed as if nothing could dislodge this man from the place they had carved for him and buttressed with their need.

The Medora Hane affair was, however, only part of a nameless battle – easier because it involved a recognizable adversary and a tangible end. There had been other crises right from the beginning. Now they recurred. Nothing altered on the surface; he was busy as usual, going from the clinic on Mount Road to the clinic on his veranda. But in the evenings no music spilled out of his windows, no footsteps came across the lawn – they only sounded in his study, ceaselessly up and down. Any relationship with Dr Schlamm was always full of lights and darks, and in times like these it was as if the dark had laid siege to his house. In our house there were stern injunctions not to intrude on the Doctor's privacy when he wanted to be alone. Once, when things had been at their worst in the early days of his arrival, I had begged, 'Can't we *do* something to help him?' and was told quite simply that the first thing to know about helping was when not to try. Eventually, as if of its own accord, a camping trip would materialize, or perhaps a fortnight in one of the huge game sanctuaries in the Western Ghats, and before we knew what had happened the dark was as if it had never been – until the next time it descended on him. But this time, after a week's pacing and before Joe's mother could approach us, Dr Schlamm himself did. He walked through the hedge (which had acquired a noticeable gap by now) and asked my mother what kind of religious instruction she gave to her children.

'Religious instruction?' my mother said, nonplussed. 'I never thought of it as that. I couldn't really tell you. Why don't you watch and see for yourself?'

So Dr Schlamm watched and learned – in three easy lessons, he told me afterward.

The first occurred soon after, when I joined a convent school run by French nuns. Within a few days of my admission, there was a problem to be brought to my mother: would I have to say Hail Marys with the rest of the girls? As the Doctor listened, she told me matter-of-factly that prayer was prayer whether I hailed Mary or anyone else – so I went and said my prayers, loud and devout and righteous as the next pupil. When the monsoons came and thunder lilies bloomed in sprays of audacious white all over our garden, I took some to decorate the chapel, saw their whiteness transformed from the dauntless to the sacerdotal, and came home stammering at the shadowed beauty of the shrine and the candlelight and the stained-glass windows.

Our great-aunt, hearing me, commented acidly, 'Take care they don't convert you,' at which I began at once to have nightmares of kind, dimpled Sister Véronique standing over me brandishing a bread knife, for all the world like Govinda with the cats. Dr Schlamm was with us in time for his second lesson when I mentioned this to my mother. She said nothing; she only laughed, but with such a curiously undisturbed quality to her laughter that things tilted back into focus, as much for the Doctor as for myself, apparently, because after that he argued less about Miss Logge.

Miss Logge was an English missionary lady of uncertain age who waylaid us on buses and even in our home, to preach fire and brimstone at us. Much to Dr Schlamm's annoyance, we heard her out every time, no matter how long she talked. 'Why do you *suffer* her so?' he would demand, infuriated.

'It's merely a question of courtesy,' my mother replied. 'The courtesy of allowing her to uphold the faith she believes in.'

'And what if she hasn't the courtesy to let you uphold yours?'

My mother dismissed the matter with a way of her hand. 'That is her concern, not ours.'

One day, Miss Logge cornered us at his clinic, where we had gone to leave some urgent letters on the Doctor's desk. She kept us there, preaching, while I tried not to fidget and Dr Schlamm waited in growing exasperation. After half an hour's eloquence, the lady caught my mother by the shoulders and thrust her face close to demand, in a passionate finale, 'Don't you want your soul to be *saved*?'

My mother stepped adroitly aside. 'Some other time, thank you,' she said, polite as ever, and we escaped.

That did it, Dr Schlamm said afterward. He seemed hugely delighted by the whole episode, but not more delighted than our great-aunt.

Great-aunt, after the founding of the impromptu clinic on his veranda, had started to thaw in her attitude toward him. She began by conceding that he was a good man, and went on to evince an extraordinary interest in his background, as if, his character now having been established, she recognized his validity to claim a past. Her final reservations fell away when she discovered he was Jewish ('Ah, then he is like one of us; he's from an old people'), and the surrender was complete once he admitted his weakness for the *halva* she made.

After this, nothing was too good for Dr Schlamm; no amount of information about him ever really satisfied her. She asked my parents all kinds of questions and set out their answers before her, laying one against the other, as if playing a sort of mental solitaire where every move was speculated aloud. It was her only suggestion of senility, for most of the day she ruled her old age with indomitable vigour. Then at night she would sit on the upstairs veranda, where my sister and I slept in summer, fanning herself with a palm-leaf fan, murmuring her conjectures half to herself and half to us. Sometimes we answered her, sometimes we didn't. It made no difference; she went on murmuring. Once it had been about Independence, then the partition of the country after

Independence, then some local politics; now it was Dr Schlamm.

This musing every night brought to light many things about the Doctor, especially those unspoken terrors behind his darkness. We knew the vague details, of course: the uncle whom he hated but who always knew which way the wind was blowing; the night when this uncle called Dr Schlamm and told him drily that he might as well get out of the country while he could; Dr Schlamm's own mystique about India and the early years here, binding though alien. One evening, lying on my stomach in the middle of his study and listening to his records, I asked him about his childhood. He started to tell me of Innsbruck, where he was born; Munich, where his family had moved when he was still a child, the street where they lived and the number of the house. Then there was a sudden silence.

'Go on,' I said. 'What was Munich like?'

Dr Schlamm was staring out of the window. The record scraped to an end; the rug smelled faintly of cat and floor polish. (Years later, when I walked down a bombed, partly rebuilt street in Munich, trying to locate No 21, that same smell of cat and floor polish was to come back, tenuous and insistent.) Finally, the Doctor shrugged, and turned away from the window. 'Munich? Munich is ten miles from Dachau. Now go on home.'

He did not need to tell me. There was a note in his voice I had never heard before, and hearing it, I was already stumbling toward the door. Two days later, when he called me through the hedge to give me a dog-eared copy of Gogol's *Dead Souls*, and three days later, when he upbraided me for yawning so prodigiously over it, that note wasn't there. I don't remember its ever recurring. But it echoed in his footsteps the next time he paced, and my great-aunt recognized it, too. She jerked her head toward the Hibinett house and said, 'Now I know what your mother meant.'

'About what?'

'About him. It was in the last days of the war. When he first moved in. I said to your mother, "What ails the man?" and she said quite angrily, "If your people are driven and dying and you are safe and alive, isn't that reason enough?"'

It was reason enough for something else, too, which had never been mentioned at home. I was looking up four-year-old issues of the local newspaper in the Asia Library, for some essay to be written for school, when I came across a small item tucked away on

107

the third page. It was brief. Karl Jacob Schlamm, the Austrian physician, of 1238 Mount Road, had been admitted to the General Hospital after he had taken an overdose of sleeping pills. His condition was reported satisfactory.

I stared at it, uncomprehending, and when Dr Schlamm came to dinner that night, I stared at him as well. It was hard to merge the man in the newpaper column with the man sitting across from me at table. Our great-aunt's endless curiosities and conclusions, the Doctor's own darkness, and now this, gathered together, emerging from the background into a cumulative effect of horror and tragedy that made his image somehow indistinct.

I was squinting at him, trying to focus, when his voice broke through. 'Why are you staring at me, young woman?'

Taken aback, I said nothing. So he repeated the question, and I was overcome with inexplicable guilt and yelled, 'I'm *not* staring!' at the top of my voice.

'Sh-h-h,' he said. 'Ladies don't shout.'

At that, I thought he had begun to be recognizable again. This was the Dr Schlamm who inspected my nails and improved my mind and dabbed mercurochrome on scratched knees, while holding forth sternly on the unseemliness of young ladies' climbing trees.

It was the same man, but something had changed. Studying him more covertly across the table, I saw the change: not in him but in the burden of my new knowledge of him. There was now a dim, incipient realization that if Dr Schlamm brought out the hoyden in me, he brought out the serenity in my mother. When he was among us, he gave us back ourselves, mirrored but somehow accented, refracted, so that my father was stronger than ever, my sister more unlimnable, our great-aunt more opinionated. It was the opposite face of the same thing that held us back, however close we felt toward him, from referring to him as a part of the family. We might love him or grieve with him or feel the palpable weight of his guilt on our shoulders, but Dr Schlamm carried an uncompromising loneliness with him that demanded a reticence between us. He seemed to imply all the time that no matter how valid our own sorrows, our own understanding, our lives had been rooted in our land for centuries and we could not really begin to know.

Sometimes this emerged directly, as in arguments with our great-aunt over the refugee problem in North India, when he accused her of not even knowing the meaning of the word 'dispossessed'. Sometimes it was more oblique, as when I caught him by the hedge the following morning, staring up at our house. Asked what he was looking for, he tweaked my braids and scowled and said, 'It wasn't only your father who saved my life, damn it.' He sounded more angry than anything else, but I accepted that, as I accepted most of his remarks, with a margin left for future cogitation. Having Dr Schlamm next door had become part of the bewildering business of growing up, of learning to fill in blanks that one hadn't even known existed. This statement now could probably be construed – or misconstrued; it didn't matter which – either the next day or the next month or the next year. Where Dr Schlamm was concerned, nothing was ever really finished; there would always be threads and echoes, ravelled or reappearing, to be tied up in retrospect or matched to a subsequent discovery. So that when he went on to say he was going away to Edinburgh for a couple of years, I did not believe him at first.

'You're what?'

'Leaving. Edinburgh. You know, in Scotland?'

'Of course I know, in Scotland. But why?'

It turned out to be a matter of a specialized medical degree – one he had already. The Indian government at that point of political turnover did not recognize the degree from Munich, so it had to be Edinburgh. I turned and stared at the Hibinett house, suddenly bleak and bereft, knowing for the first time what it was to miss someone who was standing next to you, so close you could hear him breathe; then wishing there was a tamarind to offer him, to divert his attention; then asking him gruffly if my parents knew.

'Yes, they know, but I wanted to tell you myself. I'll be back. It's only two years.'

'That's a long time.'

'When you haven't begun to tread your teens, yes. When you're riding your thirties, no. I'll be back before you know it. You'll see. Just two years.'

It might have been two hundred for all the farewell gestures from the neighbourhood. Dr Schlamm's portly Moslem landlord arrived on his doorstep with a noble suggestion that the next tenants be confined to a two-year lease, so that the Hibinett house could wait for the Doctor when he returned. Joe got more drunk than ever. His mother wept copiously on hearing of the Doctor's departure and refused to leave the two rooms behind the courtyard, preferring, she said, to wait for him as the house did. Our great-aunt, of course, filled two biscuit tins full of *halva*. The rajah and his lady offered to look after Toni. The auctioneers presented him with a massive mahogany whatnot, so heavy it had to be left behind. And finally a deputation of patients arrived at the railway station with garlands of jasmine and marigolds, to give him a royal send-off.

He was travelling to Bombay to catch a P&O liner, but kept reiterating, as if it were some obscure kind of promise, that the Madras seafront was the most beautiful he had ever seen, and that he would never forget the day he first sailed into the harbour. His fellow travellers surged around us, bristling with tightly strapped holdalls and tiffin carriers gleaming brassily beneath the station light. Porters trundled wheelbarrows right into our ankles; vendors thrust laden wooden trays under our noses, screaming panegyrics to soft drinks and cigarettes, betel leaves and magazines. Dodging each as he came by, we stood and gazed up at the Doctor's spectacled face, framed embarrassedly over his garlands in the dusty square outline of the train window.

'Write to me,' he kept saying at intervals, and then reached out to tweak my braids in the familiar gesture. 'And you, remember to say goodbye to your sister from me. And for God's sake, finish *Dead Souls*.'

My sister was away at college. Before I could begin to nod, the clamour of the station was wiped out by a single shriek from the engine whistle, and Dr Schlamm's carriage started to lurch forward. We watched the train until it had dwindled to a receding dot and then went home in silence.

The silence lasted underneath for a year and a half in an unspoken anxiety about the Doctor, while we remembered the rickety bicycle or laughed over the rascally Joe. Old acquaintances of ours moved into the Hibinett house, but I always thought of them as intruders; they 'visited' us, walking sedately through the front gate and down our drive. The sounds that issued from the Hibinett house were equally commonplace. There were no noises to startle the night, no symphonies, no cries for straying cats or countries left behind.

At the end of the first year, my sister was married. Dr Schlamm did not react to that as I imagined he would. He seemed rather vague – sent her a charming letter and spoke of cutting cords. I graduated from skirts to saris with all the attendant implications of trying to move gracefully in new awareness as one tried to move gracefully in grown-up clothes. Meanwhile, letters from the Doctor continued to trickle in, written on long, narrow strips of paper rather like the discarded edges of new sets of postage stamps, on which his crabbed handwriting descended in jagged steps to tell us of his English landlady and what I'd considered to be the outmoded cliché of a rooming house smelling of boiled beef and cabbage. Sometimes a more disturbing phrase jangled: 'Living there, next door to you, was all right. Here in Europe the horror comes too close.' Then the inconsequentialities closed smoothly in again. In return, we sent him joint family missives – long, chatty, and disconnected. When my turn came, I wrote primly of things seen and done; the important things had to wait and be spoken in person. Look, I told him, my nails are manicured and I finished *Dead Souls*, but I climb all the trees I want.

Then on a summer evening just two months short of the second year, the slap of the newspaper sounded, falling against the doormat, and the newsboy crunched his way out of the gate as usual. I dashed out to the front steps from sheer habit, shuffling cursorily past the political items to get to the cartoon. That was when his name sprang out from a blur of print. It was a brief paragraph again, and on the third page again: a report of the death in Edinburgh of Dr Karl Jacob Schlamm, of 1238 Mount Road. Later, we heard the facts – that he had gone to the music festival, that he had listened to a Wagner concert, that he had come home and put a bullet through his head. The world braked to a stop; I could neither move nor breathe, standing on the doormat trembling and trying to call out. When they took the paper from my hand, part of the business of growing up was over and nothing could be the same again, either for me or for the rest of the neighbourhood.

The auctioneers were closed on the following Sunday, 'In memory of Dr Karl Jacob Schlamm.' As if in an appropriate coda to the question he had asked my mother about religion, our great-aunt observed the Hindu ritual of his death anniversary, cooking his favourite food and giving it away in charity; Joe's mother offered her prayers in church; the landlord offered his at the mosque. The runny-nosed two-year-olds who had come to the clinic on the veranda cried, whether from grief or hunger. And nobody ever used the hedge. The gap was soon overgrown, and scratched across with tentative new twigs: a bedraggled testament to the coming and the going between us.

Mauna

Our grandmother did to silence what inflections do to a voice. On the first day of every week, she fasted, abstaining from food for physical discipline. On the sixth day of every week, she took *mauna* – the vow of silence – abstaining from speech for spiritual discipline. At least that was how it worked in theory. But somewhere along the way, the very word '*mauna*' abandoned its chiselled Sanskrit precision and eased itself comfortably into the vagaries of our grandmother's existence.

If we ever argued with her about the complications her silence created in family crises, she had one unfailing reply: 'Ask Vimalabai. She'll tell you.' Vimalabai was Grandfather's widowed sister and our grandmother's earliest champion. She staunchly defended the concept of *mauna*, even though she had no use for it herself, and wrote indignant letters to everybody concerned from the central-Indian town where she worked as a schoolmistress. Beside our broad and placid grandmother, Vimalabai always seemed shriller and sharper and smaller than ever, as if their sizes as well as their dispositions gave them enough leeway to move companionably around one another within the demands of their separate lives. The two sisters-in-law had gone to primary school together after the turn of the century. Every time they met, they talked of this shared childhood, and whenever Grandfather heard them he punctuated their reminiscences with a disbelieving sniff or two.

Grandfather's family, of whom Vimalabai was the youngest member, had lived in a village on the west coast, near Mangalore. Grandmother arrived there as a child bride when she was eight, and played hopscotch with her sister-in-law (they wore identical skirts and their hair hung down their backs in tight oiled braids), while her husband went to a boys' school and ignored them both in lordly fashion. The wedding ceremonies had taken a whole month,

113

performed a little at a time during the auspicious hours each day. On the final afternoon, the officiating priest, a pompous and sour-mouthed man, had yelled at the two girls for eating fruit that had been set apart for a ritual blessing. Vimalabai, who specialized in vendettas, went out into the fields and returned with a dead water rat, which she put in the middle of the priest's mat. The priest had just finished his purifying bath, washing off all defiling contact from his person, to perform the sacred ceremonies. He arrived on the scene too pompous to notice what he was sitting on until he sat on it. There had been a general uproar. Vimalabai was scolded and disgraced and banished to the back veranda. After this, our grandmother said, the rest of the afternoon was a blur to her. She had waited until the coast was clear between ceremonies and then sneaked some sweetmeats from the wedding feast and taken them to her sister-in-law. Which meant that the bride was nowhere to be seen when they wanted her for the second half of the ceremony, so there had been an uproar all over again, and this time both girls were scolded and disgraced. 'What a wedding,' the two of them always said, shaking their heads. 'What a wedding, It was like a circus.'

Whether the bridegroom thought it was a circus, too, nobody knew. He had shrugged his womenfolk impatiently off his shoulders and taken his middle school examinations. A year or two later, when Vimalabai was married and went to live in another village, our grandmother was left alone. Every day, after she finished the morning's household duties to her mother-in-law's satisfaction, she went to the village pond near their house and played 'ducks-and-drakes' by herself for hours together. One afternoon, her husband appeared on the path behind her during his lunch recess, and his eyebrows went up, meaning 'Girls don't know how to throw. Here. Let me show you.' So he showed her, and she was too embarrassed to say anything until she finally managed to send a pebble skimming twice across the mosquito-ridden surface of the water; then they made friends.

It had been like that for a space – five years? six years? – and then she was no longer a child. When a scholarship to Madras University bore her husband away from the village, she went with him to the east coast and learned how to keep house on her own. When more scholarships took him abroad for advanced research in biology, she stayed home minding the children: four of her own and three motherless girls belonging to her husband's brother.

114

The youngest of those three nieces by marriage was my mother. Once she entered the picture and I heard the stories about her childhood in the big house with them, our grandparents acquired a new pattern for me. I always saw them as two parallel lines running side by side and never quite meeting – until that first lot of children arrived, my mother among them. Then our grandparents seemed to slant toward each other, to meet at last at some point overhead: steadying one another to shelter others. In my mind, they were like a child's drawing of a house – two straight lines to make the walls, two slanting ones to make the roof. I mentioned this to my mother one day.

'No,' my mother said. 'They weren't quite like that. They were very close in those days.'

'Like you and Father?' I asked.

She paused, recognizing as well as I did the uniqueness of a marriage like her own. 'No, perhaps not. But they truly gave us a home, so I could learn how to give you one as best I could. Any complaints?'

'None,' I admitted, grinning at her. Here I saw our grand-mother's other pattern, this one linking itself to the women of the family, and still unrolling a little further with each new generation, like a giant carpet whose final scheme we would never know.

When I first saw our grandmother, she was already whitehaired. Technically, of course, she was my great-aunt. But she had become 'our grandmother' to the entire youngest generation in our clan for the simple reason that she was the focal point of our Divali holidays every year, when we gathered at her house to light the festival lamps and explode firecrackers in her back yard; she was the only person in all the noise to retain her implacable serenity. Besides, in that house the family did not consist merely of our grandmother's own children and grandchildren (she had four of each). There were always other relatives – visiting relatives like ourselves, who stayed for a week or a weekend; dispossessed relatives, who had to be accommodated until they found themselves a house or a flat; troubled relatives, who had to be given harbour for unspecified periods and unspoken reasons until they were well enough or whole enough to leave. On my first visit, when I was four or five, I kept slamming blindly into cousins and uncles and aunts in and out of the dark old rooms till finally the only refuge I could find was the broom cupboard under the stairs, where our grandmother saw me hiding and said calmly, 'That's our shy one.' She could pronounce a judgment and absolve you of its effects at the same time. I emerged from my retreat then and stared up at the old woman, whose face, even seen gauntly upward-angled, remained gentle. After that, my panic subsided.

Later, when I was older, it was easier to peel off the layers of voices and footsteps and smells, and distinguish beneath the constant thrumming activity in the house a certain core of quiet. On our second visit, I traced it to the shrine: a small room off the back veranda, with an array of sculptured images at one end, where the undisturbed shadows, which the oil lamp never probed, and the faint curling fragrance of a single stick of incense combined to offer a sense of either piety or privacy – whichever was more necessary at the moment. This was where our grandmother sat in meditation for half an hour every evening, cross-legged on the bare floor, her back, glimpsed through the window, very straight and still. Here the sounds of the household washed up against the walls but did not intrude, and after a while I began to realize that what I felt was not so much this excluding quiet as an intimate one, threaded through and stringing together all the familiar shoving and shouldering of a joint family home.

It was a quiet that survived the clamour of cousins returning from the playground flinging their cricket bats in a corner and filling the house with the animal smell of sweating boys; the shrillness of aunts haggling with the vegetable vendor at the back door or scolding their children; the tinkling of the women's bangles and the rustling of the men's newspapers. It survived even the creaking of the gate with the daily and seasonal visits of the household's auxiliaries – the milkman and the newsboy, the woman who sold butter and eggs, the man who sharpened knives and carded cotton for pillows and mattresses, the silk merchant from Kancheepuram, and the grasscutters from surrounding villages who arrived in droves after the rains, descending on the back lawn and carrying away fresh headloads of fodder for their cattle every week.

If the quiet could survive all this, I decided its source must lie in the kind of person our grandmother was. So I went in search of her and found her on the front steps, arguing with her son about a crimson prayer rug he wanted to put down in the shrine, to protect her from the cold of the floor.

'But Naresh, it's only for half an hour a day. I don't even notice the bare floor when I'm meditating.'

116

'Then you won't notice the rug, either.'

'But it's so *prickly*, child.'

'Come now, how can you say that when you haven't given it a chance? Try it just once. Please, before your rheumatism gets any worse this monsoon. This is from Ellore. Feel it. You couldn't get a finer weave anywhere in the south. And even supposing it is a little prickly. What's one prickly carpet against all those nails that sadhus keep sitting on in foreign cartoons?'

'I don't see what foreign cartoons have to do with me. Or nails either, for that matter.' She paused, arrested. Our grandmother's conversations with her younger son always culminated in her sitting on the front steps with a bowl of vegetables or her household accounts lying forgotten on her lap while she marvelled at some new fact he had brought her from the world outside her front door. 'I'd no idea they drew sadhus sitting on nails. I've seen only three – no, four – foreigners in my life, and not one was a cartoonist. I'm positive. I remember, because the tall one walked into our shrine with his shoes on, saying he was interested in South Indian bronzes and wanted to see our Nataraj. A friend of your father's – a zoologist, was it? That's right, a zoologist. Though what a zoologist should want with bronzes I can't think.'

She had lapsed into a pleasant conversational tone that lay as lightly on her eyelids and her voice as the evening sunlight gilding the steps where she sat. But Naresh would not be sidetracked. He waved a bony forefinger at her. 'I'm putting this in the shrine – you hear? And from now on you *use* it – you hear?'

Our grandmother looked up meekly at her son and nodded and began to laugh. Naresh never had to try very hard to make his mother laugh; she found him inordinately amusing no matter what he said. As I watched from the doorway, they seemed to fall naturally into a sort of queen-and-jester relationship. It was as if Naresh teased his mother into laughing with him at all the traditions she herself could never deride, because it was her duty to uphold them. Not that the idea of derision would have occurred to her; our grandmother's own sense of tradition was so deep that a few escaping bubbles of laughter above could not disturb the stubborn truth below. From her point of view, Naresh possessed the intelligent man's right to irreverence. So when he treated her like a contemporary, it was with the loved and accepted knowledge that she was not – that he could allow her into his world because he could recognize the grace and limitations of hers. He would solemnly offer to teach her how to pole-vault, or explain the quantum theory, and reduce her to helpless chuckles each time. Once, I heard him teasing his mother about a picture in *Life* of a famous South Indian temple to which she had gone on a pilgrimage. The camera had caught her, absorbed and beautiful, in a corner of the glossy American page. '*Life* magazine, indeed,' Naresh had said then. 'You'll be a Hollywood movie star next.' Our grandmother had looked at the incongruity of herself – sixty and whitehaired with a huge, wifely spot of red *kumkum* on her forehead, nine yards of sari draped, orthodox fashion, around a body that had broadened without apology in the bearing of children – set in some tinselly, barelegged place called Hollywood, and she had laughed until she choked.

'She never lets *us* laugh at her like that,' our aunts, Naresh's twin sisters, complained. But then they were rather stodgy and always complained. Their oldest brother, Amrith, was away most of the time, a doctor stationed in a northern Army hospital, remote even in his legendary good looks. And Grandfather's evenings at home were barometric readings of his days at the university: preoccupied when heading research projects, peppery when tackling administrative problems. So when Naresh crossed the tacit boundary of respect between generations to make his mother laugh, their laughter together held a complicity that no one else either could or would share.

Obediently, our grandmother sat on the crimson prayer rug evening after evening, until her son left town to continue his graduate work in an engineering school up north. Then she sent for the priest with the squeaky voice.

This priest was a little man, cheerful and unobtrusive except when he opened his mouth, and much beloved by all the Saraswath Brahman families in the neighbourhood. They insisted on his officiating at most of the religious ceremonies – if not for anything else, at least to tell the story of his encounter with the police during the Quit India movement against the British in 1942. The priest had been in Bombay then, living placidly in the middle of the turbulent city with riots and dock explosions going on all around him while he observed one of his periodic vows of silence when he would not utter a word for months, or even a year on end. One evening, when the riots were at their worst, he had gone out after curfew to fetch some milk from a neighbouring dairy. On his way back, the police had caught him and asked questions. To all of these the priest, of course, being in *mauna*, had said nothing at all, with the result that he was hauled off to jail for six months. Fortunately, his sentence ended before his silence did, so he was one of the bona-fide priests around with a bona-fide police record, of which he was justifiably proud.

Now, as our grandmother confided her problem to him, he sat meditatively tweaking the sacred thread that hung diagonally around him from left shoulder to right hip, and came up with a predictable solution. '*Mauna*,' he said. Since the rug was undeniably prickly and Naresh undeniably stubborn, she could salve her conscience and placate her son with an alternative discipline: maintain one day of silence every week instead of half an hour a day on a prickly rug.

We grandchildren watched her avidly through her first Saturday to see if she would give way or forget, almost convinced that she would *look* different, weighted down with silence. But she came downstairs as usual and merely went through the orderly rhythm of her housework without a word. Our cousins, who had deserted their cricket bats in honour of the occasion, descended to all sorts of slapstick to weaken her into laughter – always her most vulnerable defence. She chuckled all right, but soundlessly. Then the cook spilled boiling water on his arm and needed prompt ministration; visitors arrived to pay a formal call; the younger children scrambled into a fight and ran screaming to her for solace and justice.

Grandfather looked at his wife and said he didn't see the point of it all. 'Silence implies tranquillity, a certain withdrawal to replenish oneself. Look at you – still in the thick of things.'

Our grandmother waited until next morning when she could speak again and said that was precisely the point; it was the test of true *mauna* to carry out her duties and still maintain an inner silence ringed by outer demands.

Grandfather said it sounded very dubious to him.

As if to underline his objections, she ran into trouble the very next time she happened to be alone in the house on a Saturday. She told us afterward that she was sitting on the front steps, having just put on her reading glasses to magnify the small print as she laboured through the second book of the Upanishads, when the coconut vendor hailed her from the gate. She nodded in response, so he walked in, carefully taking the basket off his head and lowering it on to the veranda for her inspection. Then he unwound his turban and squatted down, awaiting her verdict. This was becoming standard

119

procedure with street vendors on Saturdays. Those who knew about her *mauna* were patient with her; those who didn't concluded she was a deaf-mute and bargained with her in sign language over the amount to be paid for each purchase. If they held up eight fingers, she held up four. They shook their heads and held up seven; she shook hers and made it five, after which the item was sold for six rupees and that was that. This time, the fingers that the vendor held up were so few that our grandmother peered at the coconuts through her glasses, amazed at the modesty of his demand. Nevertheless, she nodded halfheartedly, and to her further amazement he nodded back. The bargain was sealed; she paid; he left; and then she took off her glasses. '*Oranges!*' she told us indignantly the next day. 'They were the size of oranges! How was I to remember that reading lenses can magnify coconuts as well as small print? I ran to the gate and waved to him to come back, but, oh no, he was too clever. Never once turned. And here I am with these shrivelled little *gooseberries*.'

Grandfather said. 'So much for inner silence.'

That was the beginning of their arguments. Gradually, her silence became a battleground, a straining and shredded thing between them. I became aware of this when my parents also moved to Madras, though we lived at its other end, nearer the sea. On a blazing hot day, I walked into our grandparents' house to borrow a book and heard them quarrelling, anger stretched taut across their voices, back and forth through the dark old rooms. Only her husband could goad our grandmother into getting so helplessly indignant that she stumbled into furious generalities! 'You scientists! You can't see an inch beyond the end of your microscopes – all of you!'

After a moment, Grandfather reminded her in a milder tone that history was his hobby, even if science was his profession. 'And you know as well as I do that neither has anything to do with it. It isn't your *mauna* I object to; it's your interpretation of it.'

Our grandmother never said, either then or at any other time, that that made no difference to the way she felt. In the tradition of the good wife accepting her husband's dictates, she kept her mouth shut and her Saturdays silent. On Sundays, the arguments began again.

During the first phase of our grandmother's *mauna*, the house took on an added dimension. The stillness I had sensed at its core crystallized into a personal silence that began and ended with our

120

grandmother's Saturdays. Even Naresh, whose obstinacy equalled her own, was not given a chance to voice his protests – or to join forces with his father, who happened to be away on a lecture tour – when he returned after graduating at the end of the term.

It was late on a Friday evening when the taxi from the railway station wheezed in on a wave of exhaust and Naresh emerged, coated with the grimy coal dust of a long train journey and grinning at his mother, who met him at the top of the steps. He greeted her with news of a prospective job, building a dam for a government irrigation project, and she returned the greeting with news of a prospective bride, waiting for him if he cared to have her.

Naresh stopped grinning and lost his temper. 'Is this another of your million nieces?' For his mother was notoriously clannish and had a multitude of relatives on her side of the family, waiting for husbands or jobs, depending on their sex. She had succeeded in marrying off her older son to her brother's daughter, neatly accomplishing the traditional Saraswath Brahman marriage between cross-cousins and keeping hold of the bloodline she cherished with such tenacity. Naresh would have none of that. Long ago he had given her a barrage of formidable statistics on the subject.

So she told him now with composure that the girl in question wasn't even remotely related to the family.

'Well, what about *her*, then? Have you given her the chance to refuse me if she wants to?'

Our grandmother only smiled at the irrelevancy of the question and went up to bed.

When Naresh woke next, it was Saturday and all his outbursts only met with the blank wall of his mother's *mauna*. Still in a temper, he arrived at our house to confer with my parents, who inevitably became the confidants of any rebels. In our house, the girl, Indu, was invited to lunch and the two young people were left alone to talk things over by themselves; by the end of the day, all that remained was for the wedding date to be set.

'Shocking, being alone together like that before you're even engaged,' our grandmother commented afterward, but without much conviction. Then she turned to her son in triumph. 'So you see? It was all because of my *mauna*. If you'd been sitting here wasting your time arguing with me you would never have gone to your cousin's house and met Indu and made this decision.'

Naresh shouted with laughter, and after an uncertain moment his mother joined in.

121

Then the edge of Grandfather's voice slashed between them. 'So now it's a weapon, is it? The least of all retributions you deserve is to have the astrologer set their wedding date on a Saturday.'

But the date did not fall on a Saturday, and none of the ceremonies obtruded on our grandmother's *mauna*. The only obtrusion, as far as I could see, was Grandfather's caustic comments. Soon after the wedding, he retired from his post at the university. The large household was disbanded, our noisy gatherings were broken up, and the two of them decided to go and live by themselves near the hermitage of a famous South Indian saint.

We helped with the packing and went to say goodbye on the last evening before their departure. The place was already bare; the walls closed awkwardly over the emptiness now, like clothes that didn't fit. I saw my grandparents stripped of their familiar contexts, stripped of all the appurtenances of kinship. Even then, our grandmother, leaning relaxed against the wall, seemed surrounded by the pervasive hum of her concern for her relatives. But Grandfather sat on the sole remaining packing case and smoked and talked of the book he was planning to write about the eighth-century temple near the hermitage. He was somehow easier to understand than she was. He had always been easier to understand when we were children – quick to spank us, but even quicker to forget that he had. Our grandmother never spanked us. She had a much more formidable way of gently imposing her will before we quite realized we had been bent to it. I had thought of this earlier the same day, when I took down the curtains in their bedroom, remembering how I had helped her sew them five years before.

'This is durable material,' she had said then with satisfaction, pushing away fold upon fold of the hideous purple stuff. 'You'll see, we'll probably still have it when you are grown up and married.' At ten, marriage was as obvious and remote as the moon, so I merely obliged her with a perfunctory giggle and continued turning the handle of her antiquated sewing machine while she continued adjusting the purple hem. We worked in silence for a time, and then I found myself protesting vociferously that I detested those of our women who painted their lips and bared their midriffs. Grandmother smiled benignly at me over the top of her glasses and let me talk. It was only after the curtains had been folded and put away and I had gone out to play under the jack-fruit tree that I realized none of what I had said was true – I couldn't wait to grow up and paint my mouth and bare my own skinny midriff. But in that shifting of values around Grandmother which equated honesty with impudence, I could never have gone and told her so. I couldn't even tell myself so at that point without feeling depraved; and when I use lipstick now, three years after her death and in a country where it is a practice common as the *kumkum* on our foreheads at home, I still sometimes have to suppress a guilty pang in homage to our grandmother's will.

I had thought that, with her will, imposing her *mauna* on us had not been too difficult, except for the weekly contretemps with our grandfather, but apparently it had been harder than I imagined. When we went to see them a year later in their small house, with its thatched roof and guava orchards, she confided to my mother that this was the first time she had been able to live at peace with her silence.

'I understand,' my mother said. She obviously did, since she had now become the focus of the family that our grandmother had provided before. We had moved north, and most of the clan was in the south, but somehow or other our house was always full of relatives.

'Here it is different.' Our grandmother smiled, content, and nodded at the low, grey-thatched roofs of the hermitage lying quietly at the foot of the barren hill. The temple was invisible beyond the curve of that same hill, its old carved stone the exact grey of the hermitage roofs. Grandfather had gone there early to work on reproducing and translating some early Chola inscriptions on the south wall.

'Yes, *he* goes there every morning.' Like the orthodox Hindu wife she was, our grandmother never uttered her husband's name. 'And we go to the hermitage every afternoon. Did I tell you of the first time we went? There was a long room of people sitting silently in rows before the swami. And there was the swami himself, sitting on his wooden cot. When I saw him, I thought in dismay. This is a saint? This shrivelled and funny-looking bundle of bones? Then I saw his eyes, and they were so luminous and full of peace that I felt a little better. Afterwards, we sat all morning in that long prayer room. It could have been many mornings. Nobody said a word, nobody interrupted. So you see, here my *mauna* is the rule instead of the exception, and I don't have to fight anymore.'

Obviously, Grandfather didn't have to fight, either. He crinkled his eyes at us in his old way and said it was a good thing the religious discussions were held on Saturdays, since it ensured his wife's keeping her mouth shut and, he hoped, her mind open. These religious discussions, it turned out, consisted of question-and-answer periods after detailed explication of philosophical texts by the swami himself. The swami was very old and very ill, with a cancerous growth on his left arm, which grew steadily worse, though doctors came to treat him from all over the country and even from all over the world. The latest medical expert was Swiss, and had been sent for by the swami's younger brother – a bossy entrepreneur with a mind that rang like a cash register, Grandfather said – who ran the free dispensary and the boarding and lodging provided by the hermitage for the poor and the homeless. The swami himself had not wanted any treatment; he had even balked at a private examination. Grandfather and some of the other disciples had been with him when the Swiss doctor arrived. The doctor had sat beside the swami on his wooden cot and unrolled the bloody bandages from the old man's arm. 'I don't know what exactly he did,' Grandfather said. 'I couldn't see. But I saw Swamiji's face. The doctor kept saying, "I'm sorry that is painful," and Swamiji kept smiling obligingly in reply and looking at his rotting arm as if it belonged to someone else. That is true *mauna* for you.'

Our grandmother didn't answer for a moment, frowning in anxiety over the swami's illness, then she recollected herself and gave her husband the most serene of her smiles. 'Of course. This is *just* what I've been trying to tell you all along.'

What looked like peace between them turned out to be a precarious truce. Less than six months later, the swami died – attained *samadhi*, as the faithful said. Our grandparents were among the many disciples who gave up their homes and lands near the hermitage and left.

I wondered how the *mauna* would hold out against this further change, but did not know until a couple of years later. During this time, I was away on a scholarship, studying abroad. Our grandparents were leading a peripatetic existence all over the south, living for a while in the homes of their daughters and various other relatives who now claimed their right to return the hospitality they had once received.

When I returned to my parents' home in New Delhi, it was to find that both uncles were also in the city. Amrith and his cousin-wife lived in cramped temporary quarters near the hospital grounds, and

Naresh was staying with us while Indu visited her parents. So when our grandparents journeyed north to make a permanent home with Naresh, it was to our house that they came first.

We were living in one of the long, cool houses built during the Lutyens era. These had gleaming floors and white columns edging deep verandas, but were saved from self-consciousness by the impersonal grace of their gardens and lawns. Our garden had a medieval Muslim tomb in its one unkempt corner, humped beneath a tangle of shrubbery. Inside the house there were alcoves panelled in fine dark wood and fireplaces in every room – perhaps with a nod in the direction of New Delhi winters, but more probably to appease the nostalgia in some heavy-boned English memsahib long since gone. Because my father's work was with the government, my parents had made their home in many different places over the years, moving from one town to another or one country to the next, and somehow never having to argue with their surroundings. They had brought the same harmony to this house, but it seemed an unlikely setting for our grandmother.

Or so I thought at first. Then, a few days before her arrival, a favourite cousin of mine from the naval academy at Khadakvasla decided to spend his vacation with us; two eccentric theosophist aunts came for a convention in the city; various other relatives materialized for briefer visits; and by Sunday, when our grandparents were due to arrive, it was a little as if their house in Madras had been miraculously transplanted to ours.

They drove in on the crest of a quarrel. It had harder edges than the bickerings of two years ago, but the subject was the same. Grandfather had changed; the lines of laughter that crinkled upward on his face now ran downward, as if a weight more inexorable than that of age or gravity was slowly pulling him under. Our grandmother's smile had mellowed, if possible, to an even deeper sweetness, but crumpled whenever her husband's voice jumped out at her – which was what happened during dinner that night.

Grandfather was mopping up red hot beans with a piece of unleavened bread as if he were wreaking vengeance on his food. 'I'll tell you what this kind of nonsense leads to! We had to change trains at Katpadi Junction. One-thirty in the morning, and she remembers it is Saturday. What happened? What do you think? We lost sight of each other on those jammed platforms. She undertipped one coolie and let the other walk off with out tiffin carrier when he thought it was someone else's. With this *mauna* nonsense of hers, she wouldn't call him back. Just stood there clapping her hands like some sort of a pasha. Of course, all the rest of them except the coolie himself thought she was calling them, and they all gathered around her and talked at the top of their voices. I had to fight my way through the crowd to extricate her. We almost missed the train – managed to get on it just as it was pulling out of the station.'

Everybody except our grandparents and my cousin, with his young face stern for a moment above the shining brass buttons of his naval uniform, started to laugh. Then the laughter trailed off into a tense pause. My mother rescued us out of it by announcing, 'Vimalabai is returning tomorrow, did you know?'

Vimalabai had made her home with us after she retired from the school. Every now and then, she went back there for a reunion of some sort, from which she returned trenchant and intrepid as ever. After the first delight of seeing our grandmother again, she surveyed her sister-in-law with tight lips and walked all over the house and garden muttering to herself, 'She's too pale. Too pale. Making life miserable over a thing like that!' From the glares she distributed between her brother and her sister-in-law, it was hard to know which of them she considered more culpable. But she smoothed things over for our grandmother as no one else could have, taking over as her official mouthpiece every Saturday. If Grandfather had any objections to offer, it was she who met and countered them, and since her mind was not only quicker but moved more along the lines of his than our grandmother's ever did, the disputes fizzled out even before they had a chance to ignite. However, neither of our grandparents wholly accepted her mediation. There was a sense of uneasy suspension between them, as if the real argument had been left in abeyance and would have to be worked out beyond the limits of Vimalabai's or anyone else's power to interfere.

Grandfather sat smoking, withdrawn and taciturn, shifting a strand of the swami's tulsi beads restlessly between his fine, veined fingers. Our grandmother voiced her only criticism of her husband in a hurried aside to my mother: 'He depends too much. Even on a swami you shouldn't depend that much.' Grandfather continued telling the beads, the sound of their gentle clicking as insistent as the silence of our grandmother's Saturdays. The book he had written for the historical society had been hailed as a definitive work, but he regarded it in much the same spirit as the swami had regarded his arm – as if it belonged to someone else, and someone not very interesting at that. Immense circulars and periodicals arrived from scientific organizations and were stored in a corner unread, including a journal commemorating an award by the British government for his contributions to research. We grandchildren were ignorant of the exact nature of his discoveries, being only vaguely aware of a certain wriggling microbe burdened with his resounding twelve-syllabled name because he had discovered its existence. An equally resounding citation had arrived from London the year of its discovery, our grandmother told us, and had been forgotten in the storeroom until the cook burned it with the other old papers to feed their ancient stove – 'and that was the end of that.'

She laughed over this with Vimalabai as they sat knitting on the lawn in the warm winter sunlight. When it grew warmer and jacarandas bloomed like purple mist over all the city, they moved to the shade of the neem tree near the Muslim nobleman's tomb and embarked on their usual reminiscences – to which Grandfather no longer contributed so much as one sceptical sniff.

Any altercations now were between the sisters-in-law themselves. These were based mainly on the fact that the past was a book they had read together and each, therefore, had the right to turn to any page whenever she liked. Was it or wasn't it the young electrician, installing the first electric lights in the village, who had eloped with the headman's daughter? Was it or wasn't it in 1921? Vimalabai was too much like her brother to let the situation pass without using its opportunities; it was on Saturday that she pressed her points most vehemently. Our grandmother retaliated by carrying about with her everywhere she went a small memo pad attached by a string to a stubby red pencil. One weekend, we came across a torn-off strip of paper in the garden, smudged across one corner with a trail of spilled red *kumkum* saying, '*1921*, not 1922'.

All of a sudden, the days grew hotter; jacarandas gave way to tumbling yellow cassias squandering their petals down our dusty road, and then to the massed scarlet of *gulmohurs*. Every morning, our grandmother gathered armfuls of them to decorate the shrine – a much smaller one in our house than hers had been in Madras.

'But do you know, child, it is only in this shrine and in this house that I find any continuation of what I tried to put into ours,' she told my mother late one morning, her hands lighting deftly among the flowers, separating white from blue, gold from scarlet. 'Everything else is changing. It isn't like this in my twins' homes.'

'Oh, but we cook meat in our kitchen,' I couldn't resist pointing out. 'And none of us will fast for Ekadashi tomorrow.'

Ekadashi is the eleventh day of the moon, traditionally a day of fasting and prayer. Our grandmother knew well enough that we did not observe the stricter rituals, but I had to tell her in some way that my parents allowed us to be different, as she never did.

She did not seem to hear me – still absorbed, trying to sort out the words, which always evaded her, irritating as insects buzzing around her head. 'There is something in this house. Enough room, enough trust – something. You can talk together and be still together. I wanted all my children to have that comfort between them – ' she reached out as if to spank me. 'Though *you* certainly don't deserve it.'

I was going up to hug her, held in the charm of that smile, when she caught her breath. 'I – I feel strange. I think I have to lie down.' She sounded more surprised than anything else, and then slid into the slightly offhand, apologetic tone with which she met any physical discomfort. 'Just a little dizzy. I'll be all right.'

At noon, she insisted on joining us at lunch, but by evening she was back on her cot again. Grandfather went out on to the veranda after her, and I heard them robustly reassuring each other. 'It's probably nothing, just indigestion.' Only the three old people slept out on the veranda, since it was already uncomfortable sleeping indoors; the rest of us had our beds on the lawn, with no mosquito nets between us and the night sky. 'It's too hot even for the mosquitoes,' our grandmother had said compassionately on emerging from her *mauna* the day before, and my cousin had groaned in exasperation. 'How non-violent can you *get*, our grandmother?'

Now she lay tossing restlessly from one position to another, struggling against nausea, saying over and over again in increasing bewilderment, 'I feel so strange, so strange . . .'

Naresh stood in the hallway, ringing up his brother at the hospital. My mother attended to the mechanics of illness, mopping up our grandmother when she was sick, putting an extra pillow behind her back, moving quick and gentle from one urgency to the next, stopping only to give us instructions on her way in or out: 'You'll have to send your father a telegram; his conference should be over by tomorrow. . . . Grandfather needs a cup of coffee. . . . Tell your cousin to get the car out of the garage and fetch Amrith.'

128

Only Vimalabai had nothing to say, hovering anxiously around her sister-in-law, pulling the end of her sari nervously across her mouth. Over it, her eyes never once strayed from the figure on the bed. By the time Amrith arrived with his doctor's bag, Grandfather had moved away to a little rattan stool and sat hunched over it, unable to look at his wife where she lay incoherent with pain: 'I don't know what this is. I don't know what to do – it is so strange, I don't know what to do. . . .'

It was Naresh who sat by his mother, holding her hand, playing her jester to the end. 'What do you mean you don't know what to do? Of course you do. Tomorrow you'll come riding pillion on the back of my motorbike, that's what you'll do. Don't laugh. If your sari flaps in the wind, we can tuck it under the seat. And if the noise is too much for you, I'll give you cotton wool to stuff in your ears. We'll go all the way out to Old Delhi and maybe even eat some of that terrible Punjabi food they sell along the pavements – *cholé* and *chaat*, and what do they call that other barbaric stuff?'

She tried to smile at him – orthodox Brahmin, who would not touch a morsel off the streets – though her eyes were closed and she was gasping for breath. Across the bed, Amrith caught his brother's eye and shook his head. Naresh's voice went on, low and matter-of-fact, silent when she was drowsy, soothing when she was restless. He kept his hand on her pulse as he talked, taking the drops of Coramine to her lips when she grew worse, holding her against him when she could no longer lie back in bed. He was still promising her the pillion ride to Old Dehli when the pulse stopped and her hand was laid back on the sheet.

For a while after that, she was still our grandmother, lying motionless in bed, the big spot of *kumkum* a bright living red on her forehead. And we stood around her, held together, just as motionless. Afterwards, I remembered how still the night had been and how easily it had contained the living and the dead. Then my mother leaned forward to ease the extra pillow from beneath our grandmother's head and gently lifted the other hand, which was dangling over the edge of the cot. The numbness gave way, hardening into a recognition of finality. Grandfather hunched lower over his stool. Naresh broke away and walked off into the darkness of the garden, where our empty beds stood ghost white on the grass.

Well before dawn, the activity began; custom and the accoutrements of death claimed our grandmother. Against a background of

129

telegrams and telephone calls, the gathering of relatives and the summoning of priests, Vimalabai said shrilly, 'Tie up her head or the jaw will drop.' Instead of giving her a sedative, Amrith merely nodded and started to wind a bandage around his mother's face from above the head to below the chin. He did it skilfully, as if in the very fact of his practised hands he had somehow averted himself from his task. Even the carefully uninflected, professional tone of his explanation to us – the younger ones, the lay people, who had asked for no explaining at all – became a private act of absolution. 'It'll have to do for the moment. We have to make sure the mouth is closed when rigor mortis sets in.' Much later in the morning, when they removed the bandage, her mouth stayed closed – calm and obdurate and gone.

In one of the clutching impulses to retrieve a presence through remembered likes and dislikes, I thought of her favourite verse from the Gita:

Worn-out garments are
shed by the body,
Worn-out bodies are
shed by the dweller
within the body . . .

and suddenly it was quite natural that in both the grotesque bandage and the beautiful mouth she should be irretrievable. It was a characteristic absence; you found yourself fighting it and failing; much as you had fought and failed against all her convictions.

By sunrise, the womenfolk had arrived – daughters and nieces and cousins. One of the twins, clumsy with tears, tried to smother the souring smell of sickness by daubing our grandmother's sari with quantities of cologne, so that our grandmother, who had scorned the artifice of perfume all her life, lay bathed in it when she was dead.

Vimalabai, who had been wandering through the rooms objecting to everything she saw, emerged on the veranda wrinkling her nose at the unaccustomed scent, and came to a horrified stop. 'What have you done? What have you *done*?' But nobody paid attention.

With the muted gestures of ceremony, the women had removed our grandmother's wedding necklace of black beads strung on fine gold, and were garlanding her instead with a twined strand of flowers and sacred tulsi leaves. Soon any alien reminder of perfume in the air was drowned by the acridly fragrant tulsi and clusters of joss sticks that the priest had lit up and down the veranda at sunrise. Vimalabai retreated, importunate, to her corner – a widow, for whom these things were irrelevant – while our grandmother's black beads of marriage were distributed among the women in the family as a token of her blessing and a sharing of her good fortune: survived by her husband, she had died a *sumangali*, still in the cherished state of wifehood.

Everybody nodded over the honour of that – all the visitors who kept coming to sit in quiet rows on the veranda or to stand alone or together on the lawn while sunlight and the silence gathered. Nobody spoke much, and when they did, it was to murmur their sense of fitting conclusions. Yes, her death came without a prolonged illness; in our blind, comparing values she did not suffer too much. Yes, she died surrounded by her husband and her sons – what greater completion for a woman of her quality? And yes, most important of all, this was the morning of Vaikunta Ekadashi, a day of special significance this lunar month. According to the scriptures in which she believed so implicitly, those who died on this day escaped the cycle of birth and death and attained salvation.

My cousin sat down next to me with a thump. We stared at each other for a moment and then out at the sunlit grass. Divested of his brass-buttoned naval coat, he looked as young as ever, his face stiffened by the same anger it had shown when he wanted to be a pilot and our grandmother – with some obscure logic that held the sea less dangerous than the sky – insisted he join the navy instead. 'Her every gesture is weighted down with four thousand years of tradition!' he had exploded then. Now we both knew that our grandmother was so consistent that when she died it was as if she completed the gesture she began when she was born; and we sat together in silent protest that grief could be so easy.

Except that it was never easy for either Vimalabai or Grandfather. He had been hunched over that rattan stool all night and most of the morning, speaking only once. When Naresh touched his shoulder in wordless reminder of what was left to be done, he said slowly, 'Fifty-eight years.' It was his sole acknowledgment to one of the many measures of their marriage. Then he stood up, his face grey and withheld, and followed the body as it was borne through the garden, past the older knowledge of the Muslim tomb, and out of the gate.

Afternoon of the House

The river called Tambaraparani winds through the very far southern plains of India. The gardens of the big house swept right down to its banks. From the verandas you could see the sunlit shimmer of water, with the arc of the bridge lying darkly over it, and from the bridge you glimpsed the pillars of the house gleaming white between. Trees of many kinds. Pipal and papaya, a jackfruit, three varieties of mango, feathery bamboo clumps that rattled like castanets in the wind, fishtail palms swinging their tassels just where the lawn began, and a whole avenue of terminalias edging the garden wall. They went swaying up to the sky, letting the sun filter through the leaves and fall in patterns of dappled silver on the path below. When you stood there and looked up you were lost in a world of green, and if you shut your eyes the green still remained, cool behind your lids.

Mina came here in the afternoons because it was the afternoon part of the garden – the best place to be when it was too hot everywhere else. The morning part lay on the other side of the house, hidden from the river, where the garden soon stopped being a garden and turned into grounds of drying grass and thorn and snake-ridden undergrowth and old, old trees stretching away so far that you could not see the low stone wall marking the boundary. In the evenings, you couldn't venture into this wilderness without being warned by one of the grown-ups – either from the house or the servants' quarters: 'Come back! A cobra may bite you!' But now in the afternoon it was too hot even for cobras, so hot you could almost hear the grass scorching beneath the sun.

At the house, woven screens of cane and blue cloth were let down between the pillars of the verandas, the outer doors were closed, and the floors were sprinkled with water, glimmering cool in the dimness. Mina's mother rested upstairs, the cook had gone back to his quarters after lunch, and the red-uniformed attendants snoozed outside her father's office room. Soon her mother would come down, household keys jingling at her waist, and open the storeroom to take out tea and sugar and things to eat, and Govinda would return, muttering a little about the heat and wondering why the family couldn't have tea later or not at all. At that, Mina's mother turned around and smiled at him, and he stopped mumbling, because he would have gone to the ends of the earth to please her.

Govinda had come to work for the family long before Mina was born. Mother said he had been a skinny, silent boy who fell asleep at every opportunity – sitting, standing, cooking. Even waiting at table he stood on one leg, like a stork, leaning against the wall, and slept between one course and the next. When Grandmother saw him, she decided he must have been a night watchman in his last life, since he had so much sleep to make up in this one. But Mina's mother did not mind. He was a village boy from the west coast, she said, and the noise of the towns probably drove him to sleep. Then one day Govinda fell ill – so ill that the doctors thought he would not live, but Mina's mother brought him home from the hospital and nursed him back to health. After he recovered, Govinda didn't sleep like that anymore and called Mina's mother Amma, which meant 'Mother'. Now everybody called her Amma.

Besides Govinda, there was Ahmed, who drove the car, and Paliah, who called himself a butler. Paliah used a separate part of the kitchen, where he cooked all meals containing meat or fish or poultry. If Grandmother or one of the orthodox elders happened to be visiting, he never came over into Govinda's part to borrow a knife or return the flour. He stayed where he was, very busy and important and quiet, until one of the elders remarked approvingly to Amma, 'Ah, so you have separated the non-vegetarian side of the cooking? That's a relief. It's a pity your husband has to entertain so much – but if you *have* to feed foreigners I suppose you must give them the sort of food they are used to.' Amma always smiled then, but said nothing.

Mina knew that once, long ago, when her father had won a scholarship to study abroad, his uncle had prayed at the family shrine that something should happen to prevent the trip, so that Father wouldn't have to cross the seas and lose his caste. But Father had crossed the seas all right, and eaten meat, and so did his family now. The uncle was dead these many years, and his sisters, the great-aunts, only sighed and shook their heads and said the world was changing. They were glad all the same that the kitchen had a clean vegetarian section presided over by Govinda ('And he's a better Brahman than all the rest of us put together,' Father reminded them often, making no bones about it), so that they need not worry about eating impure or unclean food when they came over for a visit.

'Clean, ha?' Paliah mumbled to Mina. 'What's all this fuss about clean and not clean?' Paliah hated baths on principle, and ate raw onions and smelled horribly when he came close to you.

'Aren't you ashamed?' Amma would scold him gently. But Paliah only grinned, his teeth flashing white and unabashed in his shiny dark face. However, since he also respected her very much, to oblige her he went home and bathed – on one occasion, not being used to baths, catching a cold, which led to pneumonia, which meant he had to be hospitalized. When he returned, very happy to be back, Father asked him, 'Well, aren't you dead yet?' And Paliah grinned broadly and replied, 'No, sir, not yet.' Father and Paliah understood each other.

Govinda had lived with the family for more than ten years, Paliah for nine, and Ahmed for eight and a half, but all the others were from Tirunelveli, the town across the river. There were the four gardeners; Chellapan, the water carrier; his mother, who did the floors; and his wife, Mariamma.

Mariamma came to look after Mina when the old ayah went home on vacation. She was young and strong, her body pliant as a dancer's but firm at the same time, like the bodies of the women who worked in the fields. Her hair was combed straight back, shiny and oiled, into coils of gleaming black at the back of her head, and always she had a wad of betel leaf in her cheek, staining her small white teeth a glinting red. She swayed when she walked, and men stopped working to look up and watch her pass – very proud and silent, smiling rarely and then only at those she felt were worth smiling for. Mariamma's husband was a thin, sickly man. 'Because he also comes from a family of Christian converts, they married me to him,' she once said bitterly to Amma. 'What do I care what names they give to religions?'

But for the past few weeks Miriamma had begun to smile. She hummed to herself, and taught Mina songs they sang in her village when the moon was full and palm toddy flowed and the harvest had been gathered from the fields. One song was about an uncle who pawned his loincloth to buy a pound of guavas – 'Don't tell your parents.' But Mina couldn't resist trying it out on the grown-ups.

The servants shook their heads meaningly, but her parents only laughed and dismissed it as if it were the most natural song in the world, which took all the naughtiness out of it.

Meanwhile, Mariamma continued happy and talkative. Last week, she said, there had been a big fight in her house. Mariamma's mother-in-law, who came every day to the house to sweep and wash the floors, had protested loudly, 'This is not right – a good Christian girl like you going day after day to a Hindu swami. Don't you care about the church anymore?' But Chellapan had said, 'Mother, let her go. What does it matter if a swami is Hindu or Muslim or Christian, so long as he is a holy man? Let her go if she needs his wisdom.' Mariamma told Mina, 'My husband is a good man – but what can you do?' What can you do about what, Mina wondered. But she didn't ask, because Mariamma's eyes were bitter and faraway, and that was a look she hadn't worn since she started going to her swami.

Very soon after, Govinda and Paliah began to talk about the swami across their respective halves of the kitchen. '*Some* holy man,' Paliah winked. 'Bold black eyes and all.' But Govinda reproved him austerely: 'It is not for us to discuss.'

'Mariamma, what is your swami like?' Mina ventured at last.

'He's a fine man, he heals people,' Mariamma replied with a fierce toss of her head. 'Let them talk.'

If he was a healer, that was different. Govinda had told Mina about healers. There was the stationmaster in a remote Andhra town who could cure snakebites even by telegram, so great was his power. And the *mantravadi* right here in town, who uttered secret mantras and applied secret balms and healed Ahmeds wife when she was bitten by the biggest scorpion anyone had ever seen and nothing else – not even the doctor's injection – helped. Ahmed had driven her to the *mantravadi*, carrying her to the car, for she could hardly move. When he brought her back, she walked, jaunty and smiling, to her house. 'As if she never saw a scorpion in her life,' Govinda commented. He added sternly to Mina, 'These are good men, the healers; they have to be. They never take any payment for their cures, because if they do –' He snapped his fingers. 'Pffft! The gift of healing is gone, like that. So they must make their living in some other profession entirely, which has nothing to do with this. *This* is handed down from father to son, from guru to chela. A secret. Nobody knows how it is done, but everybody can see the result. You saw it just now – how she went into the car? How she came out half an hour later? Remember that.'

Because Mina remembered so well, he even told her his own secret. A neighbour in his westcoast village had instructed him: 'Soak your scorpions in a jar of spirit. Let their poison saturate it for at least two weeks. Next time someone is bitten, apply the spirit. It will cure the bite.' So every time a scorpion appeared from behind a flowerpot or out of the bathroom drain or in somebody's empty shoe, he took his kitchen tongs and plucked it carefully out, then immersed the wriggling creature in a bottle hidden behind a stack of old kerosene tins. Scorpions of every kind floated in the pale golden liquid, claws and legs and tails coming together in patterns so beautiful and frightening that Mina could scarcely take her eyes off them: small pallid ones no bigger than a house lizard, middle-sized red ones, and great black ones that convulsively opened and closed their claws long after they were dead. But when one of the gardeners was stung by a scorpion and the liquid applied, it did no good at all; the doctor proved a far better help that time. Resignedly, Govinda poured out the contents of his bottle into the wild grounds behind the house. 'I didn't have the right mantras to utter with it, that's what happened.' Perhaps Mariamma's swami would agree to teach him the correct words. Could Mariamma persuade him?

But Mariamma tossed her head more fiercely than ever. 'If people want his advice, let them come and ask themselves.' She had begun to change again. When she laughed now, it was as if she had a fever; her eyes were too bright and as restless as bamboo leaves, her hand trembled.

Before the ayah left on her holiday, Mina had spent the afternoons with her. Everything was quiet. She told the old lady, 'You go to sleep. I'll be right here.' And Ayah would spread out her sari beneath her head and settle down for a nap. Mina played on the drawing-room carpet with four red manjuti seeds, placing them precisely on the woven pattern and having then set out on adventures from one end of the carpet to the other. The blues were rivers, the greens jungles, and the reds fortresses, with demons guarding the rajahs' treasures. Before the seeds had finished fording a couple of rivers and battling with a demon or two, she became aware of the quiet growing. Every time she looked up, she found herself staring at the glassy eyes of a mounted tiger skin on the wall. She knew it was dead, that man-eater, because her father had shot it; and if you touched the fur by its neck you felt the old bullet wound marked by a ragged spot. But its head was very big, the mouth snarled wide open, baring ferocious fangs, and the glass eyes stared unblinkingly. Mina stared back, opening her mouth wide, making it full of fangs and her eyes glassy, and after a while everything was all right again. She went back to her game; the house went back to being nicely quiet, and Ayah snored a little.

'Ba-by!' Paliah yelled from the kitchen, exploding the silence. (All the servants called her Baby, and at first she thought it was a word in their dialect, but Amma said no, that was English, which the memsahibs had taught them.) 'Baby! The temple elephant is here.'

Mina scrambled to her feet. Outside, on the gravelled drive, the elephant stood huge and patient, planted heavily on its legs, its trunk swishing slowly from left to right and back again.

'She's hungry,' the mahout said, smiling.

'What is her name?' Mina had asked him the first day they came.

'Shanthi. Its suits her – she is very peaceful.'

Each time now, Mina asked, 'What shall I give her today?' and he replied, 'Oh, anything you like. Only make sure when you feed her that she doesn't eat up your hand as well.'

That was a joke, so they both laughed. Then Mina went in and got half a coconut from the kitchen. Though Shanthi was a peaceable elephant, there was a frightening moment when you stood near her with your hand holding out the coconut, and the long trunk swept upward into the sky and came bearing down at you from an immense grey height – poised for a second, and then *down*. . . . And there was a furry wetness on your hand, which you held firmly as Shanthi took the coconut and slipped it under her trunk into her mouth, which was actually the place where her nose and her mouth met.

'Say "Thank you,"' the mahout said. 'Salute the little miss –'

But Paliah called out a warning from the kitchen. 'Better not. It'll waken the whole household.'

So Shanthi merely lifted her trunk in silence and then turned around, lumbering, and walked back down the drive toward the gate, her trunk swishing from side to side and her tail hanging small and absurd between her huge hind legs.

Now it was not the sleeping ayah but Mariamma who shared Mina's afternoons, and she had very sharp hearing. Long before Paliah could call out from the kitchen, she would cry 'The elephant!' and, taking Mina's hand, run swiftly out.

Shanthi waited in her usual place, flapping her ears in a leisurely fashion against the flies and shifting her weight from one enormous foot to the other. If ever Paliah happened to look out of the kitchen window and notice Mariamma, he always said, 'Oh-ho! We know whose brother she has come to ask about!'

'Whose?' Mina asked the first time.

'Mine,' the mahout said. When he spoke to Mariamma, it was in an ordinary tone, neither teasing like Paliah nor angry like her mother-in-law. 'I have a message from my brother to all his devotees. He will hold a prayer meeting on the riverbank this evening.' Or, 'tomorrow evening.' Or, 'day after tomorrow, late in the evening.'

On those evenings, Mariamma was nowhere to be seen around the house. After tea, the blue screens were rolled up between the pillars of the verandas and all the doors thrown open to the evening. Then the gardeners watered the lawns and flowerbeds, filling the air with a scent of rain. As the sky turned slowly gold, parrots by the hundreds screeched and swooped and darted to their nests, until every tree was fringed with a halo of chattering green brighter than its own leaves.

In the courtyard behind the kitchen, Chellapan's mother put away her brooms and drank a last tumbler of tea before going home, grumbling all the time. 'Look at her, not home yet. Shameless girl. So disobedient. So disgraceful. Possessed by a demon she must be. Possessed.'

'She'll be all right,' Govinda said from the kitchen, his voice sounding rough as it sometimes did when he was ashamed of his own kindness. 'You go home, old one. She'll soon be back.'

But one evening Mariamma did not come back, even very late. Shadows grew thick along the riverbank; the water turned first paler and then deeper than the sky. Mosquitoes came out in droves, whining and biting. Inside the house, Paliah flushed them out with some clean light incense sprinkled on a container of burning coals. As he carried it from room to room, the fragrant blue-grey smoke streamed out behind him, furling up to the ceiling and around the furniture and across the beds with the mosquito nets floating above them like great white moths. By the time he was done, dusk had hidden the garden. Small rustlings came from the undergrowth. An owl hooted eerily through the leafy dark.

The sound lay trapped in the back veranda downstairs. For no

139

matter how many lights you turned on there, they were never bright enough. Coming in from the garden or another part of the house, you felt a sudden dank chill. 'Like falling into a stagnant pond full of weeds,' Ayah said once. 'All old houses have a place like that,' she'd added comfortably. 'It's nothing. If *I* don't know that, being so old and having scarcely a single tooth left, who does?' And she was so pleased with her many years and few teeth that Mina had to laugh with her.

But on an evening like this, between dusk and dark and with Mariamma not home yet, you couldn't laugh. It was a relief when Amma called her to come and wash. 'Then you can tell me what to wear – your father and I are dining out tonight.' Amma's room stayed warm and safe. The wardrobe smelled of sandalwood and good silk; saris glowed like jewels up and down the shelves, making it difficult to know which to choose – the white-and-gold, or the grey chiffon with jagged silver embroidery like lightning against monsoon clouds. 'The white,' Amma decided.

The lights in the house had come on one by one: on the staircases north and south, down the long verandas, in the high shadowy rooms. Pools of reflections sprang up along the floor, and Amma's white-and-gold shimmered across them as she hurried down to join Father. He was reading a book, dressed and waiting alone among the tiger skins in the drawing room. And just as he put his book down, saying 'Shall we go?' the old mother-in-law could be heard shrilling across the dark garden, up the steps of the back veranda and into the house.

'A shame! A disgrace!' She was tugging at her hair and beating on her chest like a mourner. 'What a crime to commit on me in my old age! She has dishonoured us all! I knew she would, I knew it –'

'What happened?' Father asked, and because he had not raised his voice she lowered hers.

'Sir, it's my daughter-in-law. Last seen on the riverbank.' When the old woman was angry, her neck darted out like a cobra's hood and drew back in again. 'She has run away with that ruffian, mark my words. They've run off together. Oh, the *shame* of it!'

'Mother.' Out of the shadows a figure appeared. Chellapan. How long had he been standing there? Thin, stiff, face averted, his voice low and dead in the darkness. 'It may not be true. If it is –'

'If it is, we must find them,' the old woman cried out to Father. 'I implore you – not only as head of this district but as one who knows our family and our name. They must be caught and punished.'

140

What Father replied Mina never knew. 'Come, child, your dinner is getting cold,' Amma said, and shepherded her into the dining-room. 'Finish up and get to bed soon. It's late.'

Mina hung back. 'Mariamma? She's lost?'

'Don't worry,' Amma said gently. 'They'll do their best to find her.'

Mariamma returned next day at teatime. She was barely recognizable. Like Chellapan, she would look at no one, and now she neither swayed nor glanced her eyes like bamboo leaves. She stood as stony still as if she had been turned into a temple sculpture; when a constable escorted her swami up the steps to the front veranda, she didn't even turn her head.

The swami wore a white dhoti and a blue checked shirt open at the neck. His hair was tousled, and his eyes were exactly as Paliah had described. They roamed up and around and everywhere, from the ceiling to the floor, flicking past people's faces and then up and around again. 'Why the police?' he blustered.

'Why not?' Father said equably.

The swami's eyes roamed more than ever. 'She was possessed by a demon,' he announced. 'I had to take her away to exorcise it – that is all that happened.'

Paliah leaned against the doorway, out of Father's sight, grinning; even Govinda peered distantly out of the kitchen. From the servants' quarters, coming closer every minute, the old mother-in-law's voice shrilled.

The swami was not disturbed in the least. 'Poor soul,' he remarked in a pious tone, flicking his eyes at Mariamma and away again. 'It was a terrible demon, very strong. She was hopelessly possessed. I had to chant prayers all night long to cure her.' There was silence on the veranda. 'You don't believe me? I have proof. Right here with me.' His eyes went round the faces again. 'The demon,' he whispered.

A ripple went up Mina's back.

'I have it captured. Here. Now. You want to look?'

Slowly and deliberately in the silence he patted his shirt pocket and took something out – a packet folded together from an old, torn-off scrap of newspaper. Still more slowly and deliberately he unfolded it on his open hand, then extended his palm for all to see. In the middle of the smudgy newsprint lay a small heap of black powder. 'There!' the swami declared in triumph. 'She finally spat it out this morning.' And with a last look around he followed the constable to Father's office, where Chellapan waited.

All the time he had been talking, Mariamma paid no attention to him staring out beyond the screens with a slight scornful smile. But now that he was gone she moved off down the varanda, taking such slow blind steps – as if she didn't know where she was going – that she ran bang into her mother-in-law.

'*Well!*' the old woman began, standing with arms akimbo and getting her breath for a good yell.

'Hush, hush,' Paliah stopped her quickly. 'If you must scream, go to your own house and scream. Let's have some peace and quiet here.' But he listened to the scene that followed, and acted it out like a play for Mina while she was having her dinner.

'You mean to tell me,' the old one had demanded of her son, 'you mean to tell me you let that scoundrel go free?'

'Yes,' Chellapan said.

'You didn't bring a case against him – you didn't do *anything*?'

'I didn't,' Chellapan said.

'You were trying to save our family honour?'

'No,' Chellapan said.

'What is this, then – you've become undying friends with the rascal all of a sudden?'

'No,' Chellapan said again, very patiently. 'I wanted to give him a chance to take her away with him if he wished.'

For the first time in her life, the old woman was speechless.

'He didn't,' Chellapan said. 'He went off by himself, and I think she has suffered enough. Look at her face.'

'Her *face!*' the old woman shouted, finding her voice. 'Oh God, that I should have given birth to such a fool, such a coward! Why should I look at her face? Out goes one demon and in comes another. You believe all that rubbish? Throw her out.'

'Let her stay at least this one night.'

'I won't have her in my house.'

'Then you won't have me either.'

And Chellapan packed his belongings in a bundle and took Mariamma with him, setting off toward Tanjore on a farmer's hay cart.

In her mind, Mina could see them jogging up and down on the prickly straw, staring stiffly off into different directions while the wheels creaked and whitewashed tree trunks loomed out from either side of the road and the night grew colder and darker.

142

'Hey!' Paliah exclaimed. 'What is there to cry about?'

'Haven't you done enough for one day,' Govinda interrupted him angrily, 'stuffing a child's head with all that nonsense? Can't you keep your mouth shut for once?'

Paliah wasn't ruffled. 'You are angry only because you believed in healers.'

'So?' Govinda scowled, angrier than ever. 'I still believe. One rogue doesn't make all healers bad. Nothing has changed.'

That wasn't true. Everything had changed. The orthodox great-aunts, arriving for a day's visit, thought so, too. When they heard the story, they sighed and shook their heads and said the world was changing – even saints weren't what they used to be.

No sooner had they left than Chellapan's mother threw down her broom in tears and went up to Amma. 'I can't live without my children. What else have I got in life?' And she took her wages and followed them to Tanjore.

For the first time, the afternoons were lonely. Slowly, Mina walked down the path to the river, no longer looking up and getting lost in the leaves or pausing to hop in the patches of shade underfoot. The river lay blinding white in the sun. She climbed the wooden gate, rested her chin across its top, and blinked at the dazzle awhile. Returning along the path again, you had to climb a few steps to reach the veranda. Kanakambaram flowers grew on either side of the steps, and often in the evenings Mariamma had sat here to string them together, their orange and lavender petals catching the sun and throwing a glow like fire across her face.

Now there wasn't a soul in sight. Up the steps Mina went, down the long veranda, with its screens casting a bland and secret blue shade. Into the dining-room, where sprays of antigonon arched like lace against the gleaming rosewood table, and the floor was such a polished and shadowy red that every footstep fell into a rosy puddle of its own reflection. Through the pantry, where Paliah was stacking the dishes away. Past the kitchen, with its clanking hand pump now quite silent. And finally to the window to look at the driveway and find it empty.

'Why doesn't Shanthi come?'

'It's because of the mahout.' Paliah glanced quickly over his shoulder to make sure Govinda had gone home. 'He has to save face, you know. After all it was his brother who caused the trouble so he feels he is partly to blame.' Blame, blame. Everybody talked of blame. 'Our womenfolk chatter of nothing else. Most of them feel it is Mariamma's fault entirely, how she was evil and brought shame and unhappiness to eveyone around her. Others say not, the old woman also should have been more careful; by scolding her daughter-in-law so much about the swami she put ideas into the girl's head.' Paliah shrugged. 'I myself think Chellapan should have been firmer – he is as much to blame.'

'But Mariamma always said her husband was a good man.'

'Too good is bad,' pronounced Paliah.

Which made everything twice as confusing. If, as Govinda said, healers were good men, could the swami have really been such a rogue – too-good-was-bad all over again? She was still trying to sort it out when Ayah returned from her vacation.

'Good, bad, it's all part of the same thing,' Ayah said, preparing her betel leaf after lunch. Swiftly she smeared the lime on, poured in the chopped nuts, and sealed the leaves together, spearing the clove in with a deft flick of her thumb. After she had popped it into her mouth, she chewed for a while before speaking again.

'The saint made her happy and the rogue made her sad, but they are both the same person to Mariamma. One person is made up of many things, child, just as one garden is made up of many plants, and one life is made up of many people. The swami came into Mariamma's life just as she came into yours. She may be gone now, but there will always be a bit of her in you. And someday when you grow up you will understand how all this happened and how she felt. Because that is growing. Not how tall or big you'll be but inside here –' She thumped her chest. 'Every year, as you grow older, you learn something new. Like how to feed an elephant. Look at me for instance.'

'You know a lot?' Mina wondered.

'A bit,' Ayah said modestly.

'How old are you, Ayah?'

'Sixty, seventy, something like that. Who counts?'

Ayah had never spoken like this before. Her vacation seemed to have made her a little like Amma, as if she knew without being told when something hurt you, and how not just to soothe it away but make it a part of you. Yet she looked the same – old and comfortable in her starched white sari, with her grey hair and few teeth. And as the afternoon wore on she grew as sleepy as ever, snoozing in the drawing room among the tiger skins. Mina tiptoed carefully past her and went out to the front veranda.

The lawns stretched all the way down to the river, edged with cannas blazing in every colour. A small wind like a sigh stirred the tassels of the fishtail palms, but the jasmine bowers and the dark red Rangoon creeper lay still and intense under the afternoon glare, the shadows beneath them black in the heat. This, too, was a part of oneself, like scorpions and saints and powdered demons and the loss of Mariamma as well.

If you blinked very fast, you could almost imagine you saw her – not the stranger who had stood so scornfully still on the veranda but the old Mariamma with her smooth brown face and glinting smile as she went swaying down the path to the river, put together with patches of light through leaves. When you looked again, of course, there was no one there. But for a long time afterward, if you shut your eyes, the swaying figure remained like the leaves, cool behind your lids.

Weather Report

I don't understand snow very well. Oh yes, it was exotic. As a child I always wanted to visit a country where snow fell, and in my diary – its half-written pages and the different pillows under which it was kept are lost now – I swore that when I first met snow I would eat it. To see what it felt like: on the tip of my tongue, which speaks another language, and on the edge of my skin, which seems jaded already, less than three years after having arrived where snow falls.

Perhaps this is predictable. What I couldn't predict was the obvious, that others born to snow might chafe in inner languages sometimes like my own. 'Colorado' in Spanish (which is easier to pronounce) means 'red'. The day after a Thanksgiving blizzard I am running away from my husband in the middle of this huge country, in a place called red which is white.

Buses are delayed by the blizzard, which has moved north to hold Ramesh up at his conference two states away. At the terminus the people waiting look as if they've been waiting all their lives for their lives. For a moment it's a recent mirror held up, dimly reassuring: at least I'm *doing* something now. Announcements blur and crackle over the speakers; alcoves bristle with machines where you put in coins and take out stuff to eat, all covered in plastic the way the snow wraps up everything outside, so you can't taste any of it.

The earliest practicality Ramesh taught me about was coins: this big means so small, this little can mean so much; next he introduced me to the weather reports that everyone watched, to measure their movements the following day. (At home such reports don't make much difference; one way or another, you live or you die.) So I was duly impressed, and by now I should be braced enough for cold and adept enough at currency. Still, I take the wrong bus.

The nice driver in his uniform smiles at my ticket. 'Albuquerque? I'm from there myself. Up you go,' he says, helping my elbow in.

All I had wanted was to try and get to Denver's Stapleton Airport. But most planes must still be grounded there, and any city will do so long as it can provide connections to an international flight. Finding a window seat towards the back of the bus, I decide the error is insurance: Ramesh won't look for me in Albuquerque. But how did the mistake occur? Am I so totally snowblinded by my escape that I can neither see nor figure what ticket I've bought? Did I stand in the wrong line? Or was it some computer, this time, handing my fate to me?

Certainly I had less choice when my father and oldest uncle answered the matrimonial column in *India Abroad*, placed there by Ramesh's parents. *Pretty, fair, convent-educated virgin under 23, without spectacles, caste no bar, required for handsome rising electronic engineer, 5' 9", residing in USA. High character, no habits. Widows and innocent divorcees, please excuse.* 'They must be broad-minded if they don't care what caste you are from,' Uncle had deduced.

My friend Shama and I used to laugh at these ads, I feeling safe because 'Shama' means light/lamplight – somehow we wouldn't be left in the dark. Now she teaches in a government school outside Nagpur. Anyone in her place might have said tartly, 'Thank your good fortune, being married to a successful man in a rich country.' But Shama and I have only written each other funny letters every month for as long as I've been here. I sense how unhappy she is, and perhaps she knows about me, but this last decision of mine I cannot burden her with, no matter what her name means.

The bus is filling up. On the back of the seat in front of me, someone has inked: 'I WAS NOT HERE.' If Shama were with me, I could turn to her and say, 'Slap in the face for Kilroy.' I'd soon learned about Kilroy, and Shama is just as quick with new things. It's the everyday that is hard for both of us. Someone starts to sit in the place next to mine, changes his mind, and moves on. Then I see what has been written in straggling downhill letters in front of *his* empty chair. 'Kevin was here but now he's gone. He's left his name to carry on. Those who know him know him well. Those who don't can go to hell.' When I twist my head to find the new Kevin, he can't be recognized; the back of the bus is too crowded. Oh Shama, sometimes our laughter doesn't help us at all, and don't tell me it's the only sanity, because of course it is.

That was the first thing Ramesh objected to. It began when I collapsed over a sale in banner headlines announcing four heavy-duty shocks installed free of charge. 'You laugh too much,' he said. I have no high character and too many habits. His next objection was almost too familiar. 'You think too much.' I'd heard that all my life; it didn't worry me. But I wasn't prepared for consequences, and neither was he. We knew nothing of each other, not even educational asides. He had no inkling I'd studied past the convent school; I had no idea he was still working on his PhD. What difference does it make?

That first year in the married students' apartments was perhaps the best we knew together. I got a part-time job at the Housing Office, cooked, cleaned, and learned not to get vertigo at the supermarket – dutifully seeing him off to the University each morning and waiting, ready for his return, in the evenings. I respected his labours; he wasn't threatened by mine, such as they were. He didn't even mind when I learned Spanish from Pilar next door, as we did laundry together in the basement. She told me my accent in Spanish was better than my accent in English. I told her I caught on quickest to a language by its poetry. We stuffed clothes in and out, reciting *verde que to quiero verde* at the tops of our voices, over the rush and swirl and pulmonary clack of washing machines. Pilar it was who suggested I might pass for Latin American if I wore Western clothes and spoke Spanish. 'Try, one day. You will see.' When the man at the bus counter, giving me my unnoticed ticket to Albuquerque, points out that there is no name on my luggage tag, I lie loudly. I am not I (*my house is not my house*), or Shama, or Kevin, but Conchita Perez.

Always, looking at opulent ads for winter travel where tourists can sun themselves, I've seethed at the tan of privilege as opposed to the dark of prejudice. Now my own comparatively light skin is an ignominious passport, as much to Conchita here as it had been to preconditions at home. This new piece of the marriage market was 'fair'. If my skin were darker, would my parents-in-law have so readily accepted me by proxy until their son came across seas and continents to claim his property? Though, of course, it wasn't so simple; how can it be? Vocabulary splits.

'Colorado Springs,' the driver says. More crowds, more illimit-able snow on either side of the highway as we continue south. Mountains on the right, disappearing up into clouds; plains on the left, drifting flatly off into oblivion.

I didn't know I was divided so irrevocably, or that I was so exiled from myself that I must count mirrors in everything. Has it been so from the beginning? Once I waited for Ramesh at a sports goods store, because it happened to be my first recognizable landmark in the neighbourhood. A man came shambling out of the snow (it was winter then, too), picked up an American football, oval, not round, and traced it all over with his fingertips, very slow, very careful. 'I'm not stitched right,' he finally said, and shambled out again into the snow. And I went with him like kin, while I waited, foreign and well-bred, for my husband.

How could Ramesh have known anything either? Perhaps our marriage was really our shared ignorance. Our culture told us what to do, and we listened, but we were in another country. 'I'm traditional,' Ramesh had said, first thing. 'I don't want Western ways in our house.' Which ways he considered Western and which not, or why, would take time to gauge, in a marriage that had been arranged – subsequent to the matrimonial column – through letters and family connections. Sitting in this bus now, I recognize another mirror, however seemingly alien, in mail-order brides. At the time I didn't know. He came to Delhi for three weeks of his Christmas break. We met the first week, got married the second, and flew to USA the third, with no inflaming passion anywhere in sight of either continent.

He was quiet. I entertained notions of a mutual journey of discovery, which would grow richer every year, unburdened by the illusions of 'falling in love', hoping at least we could achieve a certain tenderness and surety of knowledge. Indulgently, he answered all my questions about himself with a lot of local facts: the schools he'd gone to, the places his brother worked, the neighbourhoods their family had lived in. I tried to milk each clue. 'Tell me about your brother.' 'My *brother*? What is there to tell? He's my brother, that's all. Decent chap.' My own background was equally innocuous with facts: only child; mother died young; father due to retire from government service, etc. He was content with that; he didn't ask for more. I felt an obscure disloyalty to everyone for reflecting how things can sometimes get flattened out by what is expected of you.

Meanwhile he was pleased to show me around his provenance, tutor me in the this and that of living abroad, laughing when I asked too many questions about his thesis. 'Leave it alone, you'll never understand.' 'Try me.' 'No.' Struggling simultaneously to compre-

150

hend a stranger husband and a new country, I was glad enough to obey his dictates – not thinking of them as dictates, just taking survival notes in my head.

Television was all right; international by now, Ramesh said, and no longer merely Western. Besides, watching it was all he could do when he came home tired. This has nothing to do with sex. He'd fall over me or under me or behind me, and then fall away, satisfied, while I'd lie awake taking more notes in my head. For Ramesh, sex is what you do, not talk about, no matter how scandalously outspoken the culture around you, and that I understand. He is good-looking, good at his work; he is apolitical (which means I must curb my vehemencies); he likes television, including those greed shows where frenzied contestants slaver over prizes, and Hindi film songs; he doesn't care for the theatre or for Western music; he enjoys group outings with other Indians, and having dinner with American friends who are not what I would call friends ('You are too critical'; he's right): they are contacts.

For all my notes about him, I couldn't learn right *for* him. Here he was, taking the trouble to teach me about spectator-sports. And here I was, saying I couldn't understand why something should be called The World Series when no one else in the world, except possibly the Japanese, cared. It was worse when we went to my first football game, and I couldn't see the ball. A new and useful contact happened to sit next to us. I didn't mean to be rude or funny, I just spoke of what I saw. Fifteen giants fell on a man who was running with the invisible ball, and he had to be carried away on a stretcher, and the commentator remarked: 'So-and-so was *stopped* . . .' I said that was the first understatement I'd heard in this country. The contact laughed. Ramesh was furious. I had ruined everything. What would they take us for?

Right from the start he'd warned me not to get too friendly with 'these people', meaning the local inhabitants. 'They are too frank. They tell you everything they feel. Not like us.' I thought I understood, bending over backward to be Indian, and guarding against what Ramesh called 'getting influenced'. But then I invited a friend from work to tea.

Walking in earlier than expected, he smiled very charmingly at her and followed me into the kitchen. 'Be careful.'

'But why? This is *Ruth*. She's been so kind to me, I told you. She has a husband and three children –'

'Then invite them all and cook a big meal for them.'

'But –'

'I don't want you having friends behind my back.'

'But Ramesh –' One way he has broken with tradition is by letting me call him by his name instead of addressing him respectfully in the circumlocutive abstract. 'Ramesh, it's not like that at all –'

'Sshh,' he said. 'She can hear you.'

Yet we were never really at loggerheads, Ramesh and I; we didn't know each other well enough. When he forbade my wearing Western clothes, I had no trouble complying; I wasn't interested, anyway, though winters became difficult. At work Ruth gave me a wonderful word, *schlepp*. If I had to go schlepping through the snow in a sari, I had to find a maxi coat – which I did in an out-of-date clothing store – to hide the ugly boots sticking out from beneath the hem of my handwoven silks.

Ugly smoke-stacks rear up in the distance. The bus turns left off I-25 and trundles beside a dingily nondescript river toward them. High winds batter the trees, their bare branches scribbled against a grey sky, as we make unscheduled stops along the way to pick up or drop off passengers in the ten-degree cold. For all our confusions, that first year of our marriage seemed to run as visibly straight as an American highway, veering only when Ramesh got his degree, a grant to head a research project at the University, a consultantship with a firm, and a house on the far side of Rockville. Stricken with attentiveness, I too pause obediently as the bus at each halt, no matter how misleading the temperature.

Now he didn't want me to work any more; in his quiet way, he said: 'Don't put yourself out.' Ruth had gone back to upstate New York with her family, glad to be rid of what she called the *yennervelt* of Colorado. Pilar put a copy of Lorca's *Romanceros Gitanos* into my hand, and I put a tie-dyed scarf from Rajasthan into hers, before she returned to Seville.

Appreciative of his concern, I broached my taking language courses, studying Comparative Literature. 'Don't be silly,' Ramesh said, still quiet. 'You have better things to do now.' He wanted me to prove my convent education and step up my social graces, which I tried to display as socially and gracefully as I could, being articulate about nothing at endless and elaborate dinner parties – a credit to Ramesh for my culinary skill and negligible conversation. I could tinkle as well as the fake chandelier overhead, describing the local Mall. We were 'a lovely young couple'. 'You see, Ramesh? Now you know I can do what I'm supposed to. Taking a couple of courses can't change that.' 'Don't be silly,' he said again, pragmatic this time. 'I know you; you get carried away.'

He was accurate about that, the evening three months later when a couple who had recently moved into our part of town came to dinner. Cathy and George? Kathy and Jim? I seem to have squashed all memory of names and spellings. How I love to cook, but after a whole day's aroma of the same spices seeping into your nostrils, getting progressively more complex, I cannot eat what I have prepared. Perhaps that evening I was afraid I'd throw up my usual vacuity if I tasted a morsel of it. Or perhaps it was because the guests were livelier than usual. We laughed a lot and I forgot to be socially graceful and enjoyed myself. When C(K)athy asked us what we thought of Rockville, Ramesh said quickly: 'It's very nice. Very pretty.' George or Jim persisted, 'And you?' and my idiot tongue loosened.

'It's pretty, yes. Everything is so comfortable. *Upholstered*, somehow so unreal.' My unreality or theirs? I should have heeded the telegram of Ramesh's silence. 'Everyone's tall and blond and strapping, with perfect teeth and lots of orthodontia. God forbid you want to see anyone crippled or maimed, but I know full well that usually if I come across a person on crutches, he or she has broken a leg in a luxury sport. It seems like homogenized milk-white America.' Even without benefit of Ramesh's silence, loud enough to throttle by now, I realized I had to retrieve myself. 'I'm sorry, that sounds as absurd as your coming to India and complaining it's full of Indians. It's not what I mean.'

'What do you mean?'

'I suppose I'd just like for a bit to see a port or a place where I can experience the melting-pot I've heard about.'

The guests, umbrage untaken, kept asking questions opposing our culture and this one, and I answered with gusto, thinking it all quite harmless. I talked of how exciting it was to be in a country where everything hadn't been codified from the year dot. ('You insulted us,' Ramesh said later.) I said I couldn't believe the sustained note of self-congratulation in this town: from bumper stickers saying ROCKVILLE'S BEST! – best of what? – to vainglorious newspaper supplements. ('You insulted them,' Ramesh said.) I told of how I saw a University student swing by in his snazzy sports car to buy a snazzier pair of skis, and how he stood

153

on the sidewalk surveying his possessions as he ate a quart carton of yoghurt, shovelling it into his mouth with a plastic spoon, and saying: 'I'm gonna live forever!'

A red light at the next turn-off stops our bus. At least, that evening, I stopped too before mentioning Rockville's various and instant religious cults: we've not only got skiing, we've got enlightenment. Teach me the Torah while I stand on one foot.

The temperature from Ramesh was sub-zero as our guests put on their coats in the hallway. 'Let's have lunch sometime,' C(K)athy suggested. 'Yes, let's,' I started to say, and caught his concentrated stare. 'Thank you. I'll – I'll let you know.'

He waited until the rear lights of their car had turned out the driveway, and I was taking dishes into the kitchen. 'How could you be so shameless? We can never have them here again.'

'Oh Ramesh, it wasn't so bad.'

'Not-so-*bad*?'

That was when he gave me a run-down of my evening's misdemeanours, and I cringed. 'I'm sorry. I'm so sorry.'

'What's the use of saying sorry when the damage has been done?'

'It couldn't have been so damaging if she asked me to lunch.' Silence. Dead silence. I started to stammer. 'Wh-why can't I have lunch with her?'

'I don't trust you.'

'What do you mean?' Was he jealous, by any chance, since George or Jim had singled me out with his questions?

'You are just like these people, too frank. You talk too much. The moment anyone pays you any attention, your head gets too big.'

He slammed his way out, and as I stood with a ballooning cranium in our brand-new shiny kitchen full of dirty dishes, something else slammed into my mind. He is so careful and guarded and angry because he's lonely; I've come halfway across the world to be of help to him, and I've done nothing to assuage that loneliness. Even if I were imposing my own isolation upon him, we still lived such strictured lives in this land of opportunity. To our families at home we were 'doing well', as indeed he was, but they themselves were often so strictured by tradition and circumstance that the possibilities of personal choice dwindled beyond questions. Brought up that way, did we grow up that way? I had no way of knowing. All I knew was that I had to run up to Ramesh and apologize.

He was in bed, reading the Sunday magazine section of the very newspaper I'd vilified, and looked up as I came in. This is part of what frightens me so much: that total glimpse of how he sees me for a moment; and how I then immediately become what I see in his eyes, removed from myself for that moment; and how fractions can last. An intractable ornament in cerise and silver stood in the doorway. I broke free of it and ran to him. 'Ramesh, Ramesh! My heart's truth, I'm sorry. I won't be a trouble to you again. How lonely you must have been here, how lonely you must be.'

His smile died before it was quite born. He stared at me, inimical; had I perpetrated the third insult of the evening? 'Lonely?' What rubbish. Why should I be lonely? I'm busy with my work, we have so many friends –'

'Indian groups? American contacts?' I couldn't stop myself.

For a second the silence trembled against a precipice. Lamplight stroked his lowered and secretive eyelids. When they flew up and open, he laughed, running his hands over me. 'What's wrong with that? I tell you, you think too much. Stop it.'

In my relief at not having made things worse, I loved him for his forbearance, and I loved running my hands over him too, so the matter came to a conjugal close. Or so I thought.

The sky lightens briefly; the snow has thinned to flurries; a passenger in the front row asks to be let off at an exit, and waves the driver on. Yes, that night I imagined I would be let off too; but more and more in the weeks and months that followed, I got 'found out' as had happened when Ruth came to tea. Now it could be anyone, anywhere, any time – neighbours to whom I talked too long in a car park; a twelve-year-old we knew who needed help when his bike went inexplicably berserk, so that I wasn't on tap when Ramesh came home from work, and so on and increasingly on. During the days he kept tabs on my grocery shopping schedules; sometimes he checked by phone to make sure I wasn't gallivanting about.

'You don't need to have me on your mind so much, Ramesh. Why can't you trust me?'

'I told you.'

'Just because of that one evening? But I've been well-behaved since then, you've seen me.' Chastened, I had taken notes from that

155

lapse as well; how could I convince him that I remained supervised even in his absence? Foolishly I burst out, 'Mustn't I talk to *anyone*? There's no one I can talk to anyway.'

'What about –'

'I know, but you want me to be careful at parties, and just because people are Indian doesn't mean I can talk to them.'

'So you are insulting *them* now: Who do you think you are?'

'No one. Ramesh, I don't mean to insult anybody. We both know they're good people. There's talk and talk, that's all.'

'You are not insulting me? You say you can't speak with anyone, and you can say this to me, your husband?'

I couldn't say I could. To him, to me, to the ethics binding us both.

Was it next day that our garrulous neighbour came over to learn the recipe of a vindaloo I was making for dinner? I was edging her out of the door when Ramesh came home; his meeting had been cancelled. After she left he said nothing. He looked at me. I began to tremble, become a liar; even the recipe turned collaborator. 'I can't keep everybody out.' Silence. 'I c-can't live like a prisoner.'

'That's what you think you are? A prisoner?' When he finished his vindaloo he pushed his plate away and unsheathed my Damocles' sword. 'Do you want me to send you back?'

To be sent back by your husband: used goods, useless goods. The ultimate shame. Not because I was barren, too soon for that. Worse. It would mean I had failed, been found wanting beyond physiology. My family, my entire clan would never be able to hold up their collective and metaphoric heads again. Younger girl-cousins, coming up on the marriage market, would be tainted too. 'Wasn't there a relative living somewhere in America whose husband sent her back? Something strange about that family. Better not have anything to do with them.'

After he went upstairs I sat on in the kitchen. The tap dripped. The formica gleamed. Our neighbour's dog, garrulous as its owner, kept barking. Would this have occurred if we had been living at home, safe within the implicit demarcations of what-to-say and what-not-to-say? Or would I have crashed boundaries even there? How could something so grotesquely silly become so terrifying? Were we just two such totally different people that our enforced intimacy was driving him as crazy as it was driving me? Was it merely a matter of perspectives gone temporarily askew? If so, whose? There was no one I could ask, who might be able to span

156

both our worlds. I couldn't go to our pleasant Indian friends either, they weren't family; it would be a betrayal of the marriage tie to go 'outside', to abandon reticence and risk the kind of scandal that Ramesh, showering upstairs, was afraid I'd perpetrate. And I was afraid of his fear. Eventually I fell asleep on a kitchen chair with my head on the counter and all the lights blazing. Sometime in the middle of the night he woke me up, looking as dazed as I felt. We turned off the lights and stumbled up the stairs together.

The spring of a temperate climate blossomed outside: grass, lilacs, dogwood. He didn't mind my going to the library. Perhaps because it exhorted silence, because an Indian friend who worked there could keep an eye on me; who knows? I got very proficient in laboratory Spanish, repeating 'That is a museum' or 'Carlos is coming tomorrow' over and over again in my impeccable accent. I also read obsessively, not only books but magazines, in the hope they would provide contemporary clues about how to live where I now lived. Mainly I wanted fiction to escort me to some underlying subtlety of fact. But either the stories seemed so chic that they gave nothing away to those who didn't know already, or else they descended broad-beamed upon their own preoccupations without (for me) going any further, the way gulls sit fatly on their own reflections. At home, on the west coast, seagulls come down from Siberia in October and fly back in February. I felt as locally truncated in my life here as those birds at home. For all my reading I still stood on the sidelines, barred out and barred in.

Ramesh must have caught on to that, or something like it, when he jeered at me for my worthless degree in English Literature. 'Did it get you a job at home? No. What was the point, then?' And what was the point of my head thrumming with that bit out of Samuel Butler's *Hudibras*, of all things? FOR IN WHAT STUPID AGE OR NATION/WAS MARRIAGE EVER OUT OF FASHION? Sorry, Butler; sorry, Ramesh; sorry, India. I seem to be losing you all. I have started talking aloud to myself now, quoting all sorts of odd magpie bits and pieces, glittering and irrelevant. I am afraid of going mad. Did I say this aloud too? But the television was blaring away, and neither Ramesh nor I will ever know.

'Pueblo,' the driver says. 'We stop ten minutes.' I get out to stretch my legs, the wind stinging my face. Food machines inside and snow on the empty streets outside. Nothing seems to have changed, for all the miles we've travelled. At the end of ten minutes

157

we have a new driver; more people have got off than on. Maybe it's a good omen; maybe if the crowds thin out the weather will improve and –

A woman climbs in, accompanied by cases, cartons, boxes of chocolate and someone – a friend? a sister? – seeing her off. 'You'll be okay?' the seer-off asks, anxious. 'I'll be fine,' the woman says. 'Tell Mom not to worry. 'Bye now, honey. Thanks for everything.'

She calls me honey too, when she wants to put one of her chocolate boxes in the empty seat (Kevin's) next to mine. When she trips over the protruding feet of an adolescent across the aisle she calls him 'dear'. I've seen enough of the Forties Look, upswept hairdo, padded shoulders and the rest, but her appearance has nothing to do with any carefully cultivated modishness. She seems set in aspic in that decade. A bald bit of scalp shows behind the violently hennaed roll of hair climbing above her forehead. Jet earrings slap her cheeks; just-as-jet eyebrows lower over painted lids; her mouth is a gash of blood.

I probably avoid looking at her the way Ramesh avoided looking at me when I pleaded against hope that last time. 'I'm not asking to study literature, I'm not applying for a job, I'm not trying to "get ahead", as they say here. Please, Ramesh, I just want to take this one course in cultural anthropology. Just *one* course, that's all. I promise I won't talk to anyone, I won't say the wrong things. I promise.' What made him agree when it was palpably unlikely? Did he give it to me as a sop to keep me quiet? Was it because I hadn't been able to eat or sleep, and friends, noticing how ragged I'd grown around the edges, said so in one way or another? Was it just that the night was good, and when he fell off me he could say 'All right'? Oh Ramesh, sometimes I can't bear what I think, it seems a betrayal deadlier than my running away from you; my fear that complaints at you become plaudits for myself, equally suspect. Hiding my A-pluses from you was nothing – just another notation of how not to be too excessive – compared with hiding my friend Sally.

She sat next to me in class and reminded me of Shama without the slightest trace of physical resemblance. At the term's start the sun came through the window and burnished her head; a couple of weeks later the light had slanted further down and was gone, but there we were, still side by side, smiling at how we all gravitated back to the same place. I mentioned the word I'd just learned in Spanish, *querencia*. 'The bull returns after each fray to his territory, so why shouldn't the rest of us?' It began as simply as that. All of a sudden I was reprieved from three years of social graces; and I broke my promise to Ramesh without a second thought. Sally found it a scramble putting herself through school. 'Without the graduate assistantship this semester, I just couldn't have made it.' 'Thank heaven you did!' I cried, not explaining the fervency of my gratitude. For this part of my promise to Ramesh I did keep as long as I could, relegating everything I said to a generalized third person which divulged nothing about us.

Sally jogged conscientiously every day, like almost everyone else in town. When I commented that health had become a morality, her laughter was like Shama's. I loved her directness, the honesty with which she could cut through my obliqueness, certain formalities of structure I adhered to and couldn't quite decry. We argued, that was the point, we could argue without losing our serendipitous friendship. Even now I doubt Sally knows the blessings she bestowed on me by being not only bright and vivid and curious but familiar enough with frankness to share it. When she asked me what I thought of the Indian gurus she'd heard about, I could say they should be charged export duty to equate starving souls abroad with starving stomachs at home. When she asked me why I had taken this particular anthro course, why I was so interested in American Indian culture, I could gripe about that old and perpetuated misnomer via Columbus: 'Indian'. A label both Indian and American Indians must labour under, even if neither branch is particularly concerned, day to day, with the ignorance of that moment's mistake and the arrogance that will never rectify it. 'A kind of *mont-de-piété*, a public pawnshop in the scope of history and language, that's what it is.'

'So where did you learn your French?'

'In the convent school I went to. We sang "Yes, Jesus loves me" in the morning, and conjugated French verbs in the afternoon, and garnered a fashionable education in between. My father had to pay through his guts, not just his nose, to send me there. We financed the feast days of all sorts of saints we'd never heard about.' I did not add: 'All in order to make me more marriageable.'

Often, when Ramesh and I had had a hard time at home, paying the price for my taking this course, Sally noticed in class the next day. 'Are you okay? You look – tired.'

'Must be age,' I said. 'I grow old, I wear the bottom of my sari rolled.'

But I couldn't keep fobbing her off. Towards the end of the term, she turned to me one evening after class. 'Hey, tell me something. What's it *really* like for you here?' I stared at her, unable to speak. 'I've wanted to ask you for a long time, I can't stand it any more. You sound so independent and you're scared all the time. Scared of grabbing a bite at the Grill. Scared of stopping for a cup of coffee somewhere. Scared of coming out for a walk. We only talk a bit before or after class, and then you run. Why don't you want me to call you at home? What's *happening* with you? Tell me.'

I swallowed, sliding into my usual third-person obliquities. 'People here can so easily say, "I can't help how I feel".'

'But can you? Can you legislate emotion?'

'Well, where I come from, you're supposed to. Ideally, from spiritual discipline down. Look at arranged marriages. You keep your emotions on ice until Mr Right comes along, a Mr Right chosen by your family, your own fate, and then you bend your will, the whole direction of your life, into making it really right. Most times it works, in whatever form or fashion. I've known many happily arranged marriages.'

'And sometimes?'

'Sometimes it doesn't.' Without warning, all my second and third persons forsook me. 'If it doesn't it's my fault. I can't do what I was trained to do.'

Her hand came down with a whack on the edge of her chair, angry both at me and for me; for the first time I knew anger for me.

The classroom emptied, grew darker. She asked a few questions, I faltered a few answers, imagining I was discreet. She said flatly: 'The guy's crazy.'

'It's not that simple. With a different wife, he may not have to be.'

'Now *you're* crazy! Have you thought of going to a marriage counsellor?'

I started to laugh. 'Sally, that's as unthinkable as my having a flamboyant love affair!'

For a while she was silent. 'Yes . . . I can imagine . . . Hard enough in one culture.'

Gazing at the grey classroom floor, I wondered how many in her individual-minded culture could have sensed, as wordlessly as she did, the strictures of mine. After a further while Sally asked, 'It's bad, isn't it?'

That was another first time. I could simply, without frills, say yes.

'You can't leave him?'

'How can I? It would be a disgrace to the family, a disgrace to him.'

'What about you?'

'It would be the worst disgrace of all for me.'

We gathered our books and notes together. 'Promise me something,' Sally said. 'If you need help – *any* time, day or night – you have my phone number. Call me.'

'Call me Judy,' the Forties woman says. She isn't addressing me, she is talking to the man sitting in the row ahead of her, and smiling at everyone within periphery of her vision. The adolescent across the aisle pulls his legs in and slumps further down in his seat. The man in front of her says he is from Casper, Wyoming. He goes into great detail about how cold it has been in Casper, Wyoming, and recounts everything that happened there from the moment he woke up, freezing, to the moment he caught out bus, and all the traffic accidents in between. She listens to him, really listens, attuned to the most meaningless of minutiae and helping him out with phrases like 'wind-chill factor' when he is temporarily stuck. I admire her, then, for her patient touch on life. 'It was hellacious,' the man from Casper, Wyoming, sums up, including me in the conversation. 'Hellacious.'

'Hi!' Judy says to the Hispanic couple sitting behind her. 'Call me Judy.' My magpie head remembers a quote: Americans are so friendly they make you long for an enemy. Now that smacks too much of Ramesh's 'these people'.

We are driving through pinon-dotted hills that gently levitate the landscape between mountains and plains. A vast empty stretch follows, punctuated by a solitary lava cone, dead and black but emerging in a sudden hiccup out of the flatness. Later we pass an abandoned grey farmhouse, its windows empty as eye sockets, and a row of twelve trees planted next to it. Away in the distance a line of cottonwoods follows the invisible trail of a stream. Watching them, bare-branched and magnificent, like ancestors in the emptiness, I notice again how trees native to a soil can structure the space around them in a way that imported species cannot. Aspens had mesmerized me, my first autumn, their leaves trembling in doomed and yellow drops of light. Cottonwoods staked a different claim. Walking under a massive soaring arch of them, all Gothic and golden, I'd thought in English: 'Architectonics,' and the word shivered and broke.

I wish there had been some definite and explosive dénouement to split us apart. None. The snow kept coming down, that was all; doors opened only to close. Sally found a summer job on the east coast and planned to transfer there in the autumn. One of our Indian friends, Monisha – tranquil and lovely and *truly* well-behaved – told us she was going home on an excursion ticket for three months: would I like to go with her? 'We can travel together, that will be nice. You get off in Delhi, I go on to Calcutta.' 'Your wife looks as if she needs a change, *bhai*,' her husband Tarun said, brother to brother. Ramesh murmured something noncommital; I daren't breathe lest I break the hope. To see my father and Shama and favourite cousins and friends. To feel warm air and known textures on my skin. To look at neem and mango and tamarind leaves fretted against a familiar sky.

'Did you put them up to this?' Ramesh asked when we got home. 'I told you, I stipulated when we got married that you couldn't go home for five years. I have some important projects coming up, I need you here now.' Of course I didn't put them up to it, I said. Of course I'd be here. Of course I remembered the five years, it just seemed so long. Ramesh wrestled with the notion, he *did*, glancing at me now and then before deciding: 'We can go together in another two years.' Two years. Five years. The rest of my life, spent like dough that musn't rise, unless something changed.

'I don't have to stay three months, like Monisha. I could come back earlier. Maybe in two weeks, three, four . . .'

'All that distance, all that expense, just for a few weeks?'

'Surely we can afford it now.' I'd jumped the gun.

'Who are you to tell me what we can or can't afford? Who works for all this? I know what I am doing. You never listen to me.' I knew what he meant. 'From the beginning, you've never listened.' He went to his desk, pulled out a blue international aerogram, uncapped his special fountain pen. 'All right, if you want to go home so much, you can go for good. I'll write and tell them I'm sending you back.'

I heard myself say, 'Aren't you tired of blackmail? Aren't you *bored* with it by now?'

The room grew very still. His chair crashed back on the floor, he came looming at me, arm upraised. Then he lowered it and went upstairs and I slept on the living-room couch. I was punished with silence until he judged that the enormity of my crime had seeped into my system; then he forgave me. 'This time I'll let it go.' I sank into the knowledge that we were past goading.

I have no excuses; just attrition. And I crumble with shame, for clichés boomerang back into truth: so many have it so much worse. Technically I was not a battered wife, and nowhere near as suffocated as some women I knew of at home or had read about here. But I was finished with building my comfort out of other people's anguish.

Outside, one snowstorm abated and another began. From unrisen dough I moved to a kind of automated numbness: for once in my life, not only not thinking too much but not thinking at all, just being prepared, like a good Boy Scout. As soon as Ramesh left for his week-long conference, and before the blizzard was announced, I armed myself with Western clothes, bus timetables, and 'plane connections. Inclemency outside affirmed inclemency within; somehow giving me permission? Oh Ramesh, what can I say to you? You to whom my words have been an enemy. Far worse than the note I left on your desk, drumming up a flimsy exigency about one of the Indian girls who had to go out of town and needed a chaperone. Perhaps for a couple of days you'll be comfortable with that. Thereafter you can stand me in the dock. You'll be an innocent divorcé. And I have no more news about guilt.

'Walsenberg, next stop,' Judy tells the man from Casper, Wyoming. 'I've been back and forth on this route a zillion times. My folks live in Pueblo, Jim and I have this house in Socorro. See?' She opens her wallet to show him a picture and he makes appreciative noises. 'Soon as we go to Albuquerque I have to find a ride home. Know anyone going to Socorro, honey?' she asks me. I shake my head. 'They don't, either.' She indicates the Hispanic couple sitting behind her, which absurdly affidavits my disguise.

At Walsenberg there is a further exodus. The adolescent across the aisle extrudes himself from his seat and disappears. A single newcomer takes his place: a man with glasses and thinning hair smoothed carefully back. He wears a trenchcoat. In one hand he carries a large, worn Pan-Am bag; under the other he holds a pile of what seem to be coffee-table books tied up in opaque plastic. The trenchcoat and the Pan-Am bag go on the overhead rack. Settled down in his seat, he puts the plastic bundle on his lap and strokes it.

Lunch stop is at Ellen's Café, Mexican and American Food.

Home Made Pies. Open 24 Hours. Trucks are parked in a row outside; our bus empties. 'You're not coming, honey?' Judy asks me kindly as she walks out with the man from Casper, Wyoming. I shake my head again. I'm beginning to feel sick and fear the smell of food might make me throw up in Ellen's Café. After my co-passengers have gone in to eat, I walk outside, breathing in the cold air, looking again at mountains beheaded by clouds and plains extending to the rim of the horizon. Distant fenced-in areas – pastures? ranches? – are equally whited out. Suddenly, out of nowhere, a four-deep line of cattle appears, followed by a two-deep line of sheep, all streaking past in silhouette against the snow. With no evidence of man or dog about, they race across that white uncharted space – why? where to? – until they are lost to sight.

Do I know my own spaces? 'What will it be like for you at home?' I hear Sally asking, though she hasn't a clue about my departure. With what mindless desperation I've wrested that Damocles' sword out of Ramesh's hands and thrust it at everyone, including myself. *This* punishment he is not answerable for. How can I possibly go back now? A disgrace at home is worth two abroad – what have I brought upon those I cherish? If I can't go home, where *can* I go?

I start to shake; the letters spelling out the destination at the top of the bus begin to blur. SAN DIEGO. Maybe that's the answer. Keep travelling until I reach the warm, amniotic fluid of an ocean and regain some sense of personal birthright. Which reminds me, in my contented heathenism and talismanic need to laugh, of being born again. Happy Birthday, Happy Birthday, I'll say to myself twice; but where will it lead me? Can I ask Sally for advice? Can I get a job – when jobs are scarce and I don't know a soul on that coast – to repay Ramesh the house-keeping money and more, which I've borrowed without compunctions for my 'escape'?

'La Veta Pass next,' Judy says, knowledgeable as ever, when everybody troops back *en masse* from Ellen's Café. 'Nine thousand something, almost ten thousand feet. Terrible in winter.'

The bus groans into gear and begins its long ascent into mountains shrouded in cloud and a road shrouded in snow. Pressing my nose against the window pane gives me nothing, just that stippled obfuscation of white on grey. I can't keep sifting through my situation any more, I can't see.

This journey, Judy's prattle, and the rumbling responses of the man from Casper, Wyoming will never stop. Our lives are bounded by the edge of the bus. My head aches abominably; closing my eyes,

I can't shut out the grind and fug and ceaseless chatter of our context. 'OOOH,' Judy screams when we skid. 'That was close.'

Was it? Would it matter so much, no matter how selfish or cowardly the way out, if we hurtled over the edge of the road and fell into the ravine below? Instead I fall into an uneasy doze and dream of our neighbour's cat clawing my heart – shaped like a chocolate box – out from beneath a gaggle of skin and bone. 'Fort Garland next,' Judy announces, suddenly pellucid. Waking, I no longer inhabit myself. The numbness takes over again, mutates me into a witness, exhausted and watching, merely watching.

We are on the other side of the mountain range now, with snow-blurred New Mexico spreading away somewhere beyond the state border. Sally, having done fieldwork in this area, has stressed how easy it is to muddle San Antonio Mountain with Ute Mountain – 'They both look rounded from certain angles!' Two mounds rise ahead but I've forgotten how to differentiate them. I can only recall that San Antonio is the sacred northern mountain for the Tewa, and that ghost lights are said to shimmer at night from Ute Mountain. I can only understand, far more than I understand anything about my own life, why mountains are holy to the Indians of this land – recognizable and permanent and marking the directions.

Directionless, I hear Judy: 'Now, see, we'll stop by that restaurant. When we start out again, look for the old fort on the right.'

She and the man from Casper, Wyoming, come over to my side of the bus to look out together. The small, walled-in square of buildings stands minuscule and military in the surrounding vastness of *mesas*. Vaguely, I consider parallels all over the world: the magnamity of landscapes and the niggardliness of their inhabitants; the kind of courage that can be born out of cupidity; then I let it go.

I can only look and look, as if my life truly depended on it. The man who got on at Walsenberg unties the plastic bundle on his lap and puts the contents (indecipherable from where I sit) on the seat next to his. Then he comes striding purposefully toward the toilet at the back of the bus.

'Hi, how are *you* today?' Judy says, indefatigable.

'Fine! And you?' Stopping at once, toilet apparently forgotten, he one-up-mans her before she can ask him to call her Judy. 'I'm Dick. Want to see my photograph albums?'

'Sure.'

But he seems to forget about the albums too, as he stands talking, looped across the aisle. The bus almost skids again. This time Judy doesn't notice; she is too busy defending herself to Dick, who asks her why she is killing herself at the back of the bus, smoking. Then I realize which section of the bus I'm in, and how those up front, like the kid eating yoghurt, will live forever.

'I keep trying to stop.' She gives him a stringently meticulous account of every attempt and every failure. Throughout her recital he keeps telling her how stupid she is to smoke, and how depraved, and how wrong. She accepts it all, nodding yes, yes, that's true, you're right. How accommodating she is, after being so pushy; and is she pushy so that she can be accommodating? Now she is patting the empty seat next to her. He sits down. They put their heads together and embark on a long, inaudible conversation. Eventually he goes up front to fetch the albums. They do look like an assortment of old family albums, big and little and bashed in at the corners; I expect him to sit by Judy, annotating every photograph. He merely hands them over in silence and returns to his place.

Judy looks through the photographs; the man from Casper, Wyoming, looks out the window. In one of the nameless little towns along our route, a side street delves down into a valley clustered with adobe dwellings that remind me of the mud houses at home. Low, earth-coloured, fluidly following the line of the land, all their roofs and walls and windows bear the curve and effort of the human hand.

Struggling up with her arms full, Judy walks over to Dick. 'Thank you. So beautiful. She's so beautiful. I'm so *sorry*.' He ducks his head, taking the albums from her and wrapping them up in plastic again.

Whe she comes back to her seat the man from Casper, Wyoming, turns around. 'Why d'you take that? You smoke, you don't smoke, ain't none of his business.'

'Sshh,' Judy says. 'Never mind. He's hurting. His wife bent down on a crosswalk to pick up her pack of cigarettes, and a truck hit her and she died.'

She is speaking quite low, but Dick shoots bolt upright from his seat and whips around to face the back of the bus. 'That's NOT why,' he shouts at Judy. 'I've known for fifty years that cigarette smoking is bad for you.' He sits down again.

The bus turns right at a signpost marked 'Costilla'. The mountain beyond the single main street stops looking rounded. No ghost lights in the late afternoon; no more passengers, just parcels. The driver shakes the snow off his cap before starting the bus again. Gradually the land shrugs into steep hills on either side of the road. We pass a post office that says 'Questa, N.M.', and ease into the carpark of what looks like a grocery store but turns out to be a Trailways stop.

Dick reaches up to unfold his trenchcoat, and fishes an instammatic out of the Pan-Am bag. 'That's all it contains,' Judy informs us, when he has climbed off, safely out of earshot. 'That camera, a pair of pyjamas, one change of clothes, toothbrush, toothpaste, stuff like that. He told me.'

In the middle of a street in Questa, New Mexico, Dick in his trenchcoat with his glasses and smoothed-back thinning hair, photographs a sign painted NATURAL HONEY on the right, and a molybdenum mine scarring the mountains on the left. Snowflakes drift and whip around him as he points his instamatic this way and that.

Judy resumes the rest of his story: he has been travelling ever since his wife died. Over three thousand miles now, and he means to go on. For three thousand miles he has been riding buses, carrying the proof and remnant of their lives, collaring strangers to show her pictures to.

When he climbs back into the bus, Judy and the man from Casper, Wyoming, are looking out of their respective windows. Dick folds up his trenchcoat, pushes the instammatic back into the Pan-Am bag, and takes his only luggage on his lap. Light falls on the slant of his cheekbone as through a shadow, as on the passing landscape, as on Ramesh and me reckoning hereafter with the end of each undone day.

The snow blows harder. My friend, my friend, I want to say to Dick: I'm sorry – beyond apology, and investitures of the self, and all the alphabets of living to be relearned so painfully in the weather of subsequence. I'm running too, and to my husband I might as well be dead. There aren't enough buses we can catch.

But I have to assume there are.

Spaces of Decision. South India: 1890s to 1970s

On her fifth birthday, at the turn of the century, she is given her grandmother's ear ornaments. Forty-eight uncut rubies to the pair: set in hammered gold that curls close as petals around each glowing centre, with a row of pearls trembling in a crescent below to complete the pattern and cover the whole ear.

Maybe it is part of her dowry. Only eighty-two years later, I do not know. She in turn gives me one of the pair when I am married – what happened to the other, I do not know either. But in my generation, given the shifting cruelties of ornamentation, we don't have all the requisite holes in our ears since the cartilage is left alone and only the lobes are pierced. So we turn the jewel into a pendant for a necklace: involving *links* and *chains*.

Everyone says the new craft is not like the old, the rubies not as deep. But I think of her, my grandfather's sister.

And when I am done with marriage and have dispensed with a lot of paraphernalia, this one thing stays with me. I carry it across continents, sometimes in a brown paper bag on crowded streets; keep it in a filing cabinet under 'F' (to Fool burglars); and wear it, a shared symptom, at my throat.

We call her Radha-akka, elided to Radhakka. Our coming into one another's daily lives follows the covenant as previous and patterned as the heirloom. When she retires as one of India's first woman schoolteachers, in a small southern town, my mother writes to her. It probably doesn't even have to be spelled out: *You looked after me when I was young, I look after you when you' are old.* Radhakka arrives. Skinny, peppery, glasses sliding down her nose as one day mine will too.

With her comes my initial awareness of space around a word: allowance for flexibility, for interpretation, for whole waiting and possible worlds.

Whenever we children have to eat earlier than the grown-ups, she sits down with us to tell us stories . . . and makes a nourishment of story-telling for a long time, if not forever, after.

Not for her the traditional legends which you might hear from any grandparent. Her flair for wild stories is topped only by her flair for wilder explanations. She is my earliest myth-maker, my first neologist. Nouns turn into adjectives turn into concepts I never dreamed of, and it is all told resoundingly in the neuter gender, so that you have to guess *what* is who.

She has one serial about Thitto, Mitto and Apook. (Thitto, by some stretching of vowels and linguistic imagination, could be very tangy pickle in our dialect; Mitto could be a slangy grain of salt. Apook means nothing whatever.) At any rate, Thitto rides a thitto horse, Mitto rides a mitto horse, and Apook rides two horses. Then we have an explanation.

So they aren't people?

(Insulted): What do you think?

Thitto isn't a pickle either?

It's a *that*. Not a this, a that.

Mitto?

Another that.

So Apook is two thats?

Don't be silly.

Stumped, stupid and prosaic, I hazard: 'Sort of Siamese twins?' 'What am I *telling* you?' she yells, exasperated. 'Forget about people and pickles. Apook is double. Twice.'

(With the result that I've been smitten with eruptions of Apook-hood ever since, and take to writing no less than two letters or reading no less than two books at a time, embarking on multiple projects and juggling irreconcilable situations, even when I know full well that their simultaneity as much as my *mishegoss* dooms them to disaster.)

Then there are her tall tales that turn hyperbole into a fine art, all about a rural South Indian Baron Munchausen. Chased by a tiger to the edge of a river, and unable to swim, he shouts: 'Cooooo!' The echo comes back, 'Cooooo!' He ties one coooooo to the other, and swings himself across, hand over hand, to the opposite bank. But he has forgotten tigers can swim. This one is still after him. So he climbs to the safety of a thumba tree. (Thumba shrubs grow to a height of about six inches above the ground.) The tiger roars, getting louder and closer. He is so terrified, he pees. The tiger comes scrambling up the trickle. Just in time, he stops peeing. The tiger falls back. Dead.

After this we hear the adventures of the bitter gourd and the green mango, who are brothers, and their sister, a squash. She does nothing, she's just clasically there: first to be abducted, then to be saved, and to cook for the protagonists in between times. The story is told in the *active* voice:

A demon who abducts the squash gets vanquished by his own obtuseness. (He hasn't a chance from the moment the rhymes and puns and nonsense words begin – lexical weapons of irreverence against might, which I can't translate adequately, whether into life or English or any other language.) The older brother, Bitter Gouard, is thin and cautious, like Cassius. The younger brother, the mango, is roly-poly, inventive, irrepressible; his nature keeps getting the better of his hazards – so of course it is he who devises each victory.

Out of frustrations. Blankets so short that if you pull them up to your chin your feet stick out, and if your feet are covered your top is bare. Appetites so large that you must add a burlap stomach to your own, to match them. Not only heat and cold and greed and danger, but a poke at something else no other stories name for me.

Hers don't either, if it comes to that. She makes me fend for myself. And make a friend of her mythology, so that I can no longer speak of feeling like a vegetable – or, in a rage, call someone a cabbage with academic pretensions – without retracting it at once.

Though she has come to live with us – and then moves with us from south to north – Radhakka won't be superannuated. There's always an accessible, if reluctant, gaggle of children to be rounded up. And when after a stubborn two-year refusal to be made literate, I finally capitulate, she teaches me arithmetic with cowrie shells. The smallest for units, medium for tens, larger for hundreds, and unimaginable jeroboams beyond for anything more. Arithmetic with her is tactile and wondrously available. Only in school systems, afterward, does the dehydration, the de-humanization set in; and I set my face against that. (A friend is to say, decades later, about setting-one's-face-against: 'Not a gesture for others, but the deep muscles of the self.')

There is this muscularity in our kinship, hers and mine, since we are opposed as furiously as we share. One day, listening to a classical concert on the radio, I am tapping in time to the *tala* and

171

miss out an important sequence of beats. 'You missed,' she says. I hate her. Let me hear, just let me *hear*. Which can't be said, because she is an elder, not even when I want to shout: NEVER MIND ABOUT RHYTHM PATTERNS! Patterns. Patterns. I won't have them imposed on me, and have had to absorb them. She won't either, and has had to, much worse.

As a child she is married to a man thrice her age. After the ceremony he returns to his village; on attaining puberty, she will join him. Until then, she plays with her siblings – two brothers, and two younger sisters who have also been duly parcelled off and are awaiting delivery to their appointed roles in life. But nobody can rob them of their childhood. Not just yet.

Taken to pay a condolence visit at a neighbour's house, they are seized with giggles and disgrace themselves. The sister next in age is pretty and pampered and used to having her own way. If she can't, she lies down at once wherever she is, spread-eagled flat on her back with her eyes tight shut and her mouth wide open, threatening: 'I'm going to die *right* now.' After the umpteenth time, Radhakka eyes her grimly, bends over, and spits into the open mouth.

She is still a child, still waiting to join her husband, when he dies in a cholera epidemic. She joins instead the ranks of 'virgin widows' who are beyond any easy counting of any cowrie shells. But her father is a social reformer for his time, a wise and good man. He shields her from a shorn head and mourning white, tries to prepare her for what to do next. Remarriage as well as further education for women is unheard of – entailing, if attempted, a whole gamut from disapproval to ostracism to having stones thrown at you, to undetailed worse. He tells her: 'I know you are brave and can think for yourself. If you want to marry again, we'll arrange it. If you want to study, we'll take care of that too. In any case we'll stand by you . . . that you are sure of. Do whatever you wish.'

Hearing that handed down, I join in the general applause for their courage and staunchness. It isn't until I am grown myself that I realize the issue has been in the form of an either–or, either marriage or education: which is all they are allowed, reformer and unfortunate alike. The choices she is offered are so mutually exclusive, they are gateways to two more social prisons.

She 'decides'. She opts for education. A degree, a teachers' training certificate. She will not speak of the process involved, only of the end achieved. An earning job, two small rooms of her own in

172

a house around the corner from school.

As long as her father is alive, she goes home for vacations, or visits the brother whose wife is her favourite sister-in-law, and then rescues a small niece (my mother) who is in need of care. Afterwards, with the disruptions of change, her holidays have to be spent in the households of other relatives who make her welcome enough in the gregarious, flexible way of family houses. I can imagine it, that flexibility which can always take her in by assigning her a place as a supernumerary. She is not *part* of the household, she lives alone. Scandalous, but don't say so. Fiercely she clutches at her independence, thereby retreating only further to the fringe. If the bite of her conversation makes them uncomfortable, decorum deems her unworthy of rebuttal and overlooked anyway in the bustle of their own lives: Poor Thing. In their eyes her aloneness turns to loneliness. She is bitter with relief to be back.

Back to the earning job and the two rooms of her own, around the corner from school. The map of her life, so benignly framed with freedom.

'It was worst for my youngest sister,' Radhakka says once, sombre.

This youngest one, Sita, is the prettiest of the three sisters, both gentle and plyisically precocious. She goes off to her husband's house sooner than the middle sister does; so gentle, she is unprepared – for the 'facts' of either life or in-laws. Terrified, she starts her mammoth family with twins at thirteen. In her twenties, still so beautiful, she is widowed. Head shaven bare by custom for her shame of outlasting her husband; an inauspicious event wherever she goes.

When I meet her, she is rosy-cheeked and placid and loved, the drape of a widow-white sari hiding the grey stubble on her head. Someone tilts the sugar bowl. She lifts it up, wipes its rim, and sets it tenderly back in place. Her gentleness is intact and formidable. Self-generating perhaps – irrespective of its object, or of what the subject has been subjected to. For all their evidence, the predicates are nowhere in sight. I am awed and adoring, like everyone else (you can't resist her); but it is impossible to decipher the sentences of . . . and on . . . her life. They read almost too successfully like what my own sister calls the Sita syndrome – referring to the goddess Sita who is the epic ideal of noble, suffering womanhood.

But this Sita has something else besides: laughter. The moment she sees Radhakka she remembers the disastrous condolence visit of their childhood, and gets the giggles again. 'You were always so *sharp*,' she says admiringly at one point. 'Not like me –' Maybe that's it? In part? Later, with the same italicized softness, she remarks to my mother: 'You know, Radhakka has never known how to *bend*.'

But that is perhaps what I cherish most in Radhakka, though it inevitably makes waves for those around her.

My mother, who has so far never had any 'servant trouble' because her every gesture underlines mutuality and allows space, suddenly finds cooks giving notice: '*You* may have to put up with the old woman because you're related to her. I am not, thank God, so I'm leaving.' And I *am*, thank God (related, not leaving or cooking or running a multifarious household), and I appreciate her.

She shows me ungainliness; difficulties; mis-fitting; a continuing resentment, even so many years later, at having been made to feel by her own so-different mother like an ugly duckling set in aspic – and this in and from a place where to speak disrespectfully of your parents (especially to children) is tantamount to blasphemy.

She's cantankerous, impatient, often so transparently wrong – the first adult I know who makes a present to me of her failings. There they are, as clear as my own. She relieves me of exemplars, and . . . all unwitting . . . allows me to be critical, with or without laughter.

Sometimes she does it on the spot:

Like the rest of us, but especially those of her generation, she too is permeated with traditional beliefs and speaks often of 'time – for birth and death and karmic cycles.'

One day we are looking over our respective patches of garden. (She grows vegetables, so I grow flowers.) Inadvertently she steps on an ant-heap, is bitten, and starts in a fury to stamp on every ant in sight, killing them all.

'Radhakka!' I protest. 'Radhakka, stop! What are you doing?'

'Their time has come,' she says, stamping away.

Sometimes she does it in retrospect:

After that first week of lessons, her verdict is delivered, to be repeated at intervals over the years: 'With your brains, you should have been a boy.'

And of course she makes the authoritative pronouncement as meekly as I hear it. We are contemporaries across generations, giving us contemporaries across cultures; what we say to one another doesn't belong to us alone.

174

Not all her stories are funny or outrageous. In certain anecdotes about her own life, a strangeness creeps in.

During those early vacations at her parents' house, she encounters a mendicant yogi on every visit. He comes at dusk, usually when everyone else happens to be away (at places where, as a widow, she cannot go).

'I thought he was begging, and went to the kitchen to get some rice. I was a little frightened –' There's a half-giggle in her voice. Fear? I see the isolation of the house, with only the forest and the fields outside, and darkness gathering at the windows. 'So I hesitated. But he only went three times around the house, sprinkling handfuls of water . . . like a purification ceremony, you know? . . . and when I looked again, he was gone.'

With the rest of her stories, this one stays with me. Once I mention it to her brother, my favourite great-uncle. He is rather a Renaissance man: vet, historian, scientist (whose contributions to research, at home and abroad, are beyond my fathoming); he also puts up with my endlessly devouring curiosities. This time I happen to be obsessed with ascetic rituals, and remember Radhakka's yogi.

'What was he doing? Was that Ganges-water to protect your house?'

'Oh, that.' My great-uncle dismisses it. 'That was her dead husband. He was always appearing in different forms and calling her through the windows.'

He doesn't mean aberrations, he means ghosts.

I flounder, trying to disentangle, understand. Not about ghosts, which are a common enough property, but the effect on *her*.

How does she feel, how did she feel, unclaimed wife of a stranger husband, revenant or otherwise?

Who is claiming what?

I can never ask her. Not out of the usual respect-to-elders, but from courtesy. This cuts too close; I can't trespass.

There is a time in Radhakka's life of which nobody speaks. Blank.

Except for a hint from a thoughtful aunt of mine. But she is a generation down, so her knowledge, as she admits, is spotty with reticence and hearsay. How to tell of what you don't really know? That impenetrable in all our lives?

Perhaps it's another lodger in the same house where Radhakka rents her rooms. Perhaps not. She goes away. The family has it that she is ill and needs special treatment, an extended convalescence.

Whether it is her body that must be punished for its wanting, or her mind that must be safeguarded from hurt, nobody knows. It is all hushed up. Perhaps if 'the truth' came out, she would be expelled from the school.

'How *can* they?' I burst out. With this particular aunt who tells me about the incident, I can be as passionately vociferous as I like. Even so, I am trained not to speak of sex. Or of the emotions it engenders. 'When I hear Radhakka talk sometimes, I wish something *had* happened – that is, if it was worth the pain, for her. . . . Oh, but how can they? How can a need be treated like a disgrace?'

My aunt looks at me, very silent, very dry.

Back goes Radhakka then, after that nameless interval. Back to the two rooms around the corner from school.

She becomes intensely religious. The town has an ashram, built around the presence of a holy man. The swami is revered; he doesn't run around making miracles to prove his saintliness. Any activities attached to the place – from charitable work to communal meals to lectures and discussions – are tacitly safe and sanctioned. More and more of her evenings are spent there. (All this is a subterranean understanding between us, and never spelled out: shadows of thatch I have not seen, falling on the textures of cotton carpets spread on the floor; and Radhakka sitting there, willing herself to be *still*. . . .) Quiet and the presence of her swami.

'NO ONE like him!' she says pugnaciously, though nobody is about to contradict her. When she comes to us she brings his photograph in a wooden frame and accords it highest honour in our houschold shrine. All other gods and goddesses make way without protest for this gentle, bespectacled old man who has given her anchor: he is sitting on a chair, wrapped in a shawl, there's a tiger-skin on the floor beneath, and his hanging feet don't quite touch it.

Before she can get spiritually 'detached' into the desired non-desiring, the Independence movement gathers momentum. There is space carved in it for her, as for anyone, irrespective of gender or social stigma. She throws herself in. And here too, the guru and the gospel advocate non-violence, plus a stringently controlled temperance toward life.

All the after-years we spend together I am to see this sundering in her. The fullness of small pleasures and the austerity that must deny them. We sneak off, the two of us, to see terrible Hindi movies; but

176

we sit deafened by claps and catcalls in the cheapest 'rowdies' seats up front, prim among the peanut shells. Even as she declares her most impassioned political and national convictions, her elbow is nudged in a constant reminder to be gentle – the zest for a fight becoming a streak of malice when fisticuffs (even as a metaphor) are taboo.

Yet there's another stubborn zest that won't be stilled. She doesn't lose it until the death of her brother's wife, her best friend and adversary, whom she has championed like a cause over the decades – their companionship instantly renewed whenever they meet. They insist on reading letters together, and neither will wear glasses, but Radhakka is myopic and her sister-in-law is far-sighted.

'You're holding it too close!'

'You're holding it too far!'

Too close and too far, back and forth, too close and too far goes the letter, until is is nearly in shreds; but they have read it together, like the past.

Now she no longer wants to live. Long, long months and years of slow atrophy. The oxygen tent, the catheter. Hospitals are overcrowded. My mother does it all, beyond covenants; and the rest of us help out as much as we can, I whenever I am home from college, sitting evening after evening at her bedside, trying at times to wring a laugh out of her by telling her tales like her own. But when I make an equally sorry job of trying to thank her for the sustenance of those stories, she gives me a polite smile and says vaguely: 'What stories?' As she turns her head for a sip of water the lamplight shines translucent through the shell of her ear, and I can see the holes bored in the cartilage for that ornament the child-bride once wore.

Her mind is going, but keeps hold of its divisions, riven down to the last splinters. Sporadically she asks for the newspaper she has always subscribed to, keeps track of whenever my father has to confer with the Prime Minister about the current Five Year Plan, calling me to whisper: 'Tell him to be sure not to forget *this* aspect. . . .'

'Yes,' I soothe her. 'Yes, yes.'

As I am going out she calls me in again, suddenly sharp. 'Also be sure to put the right things in the *kurkut*, so we'll have no trouble from beyond the river.'

'Yes,' I say again, but now mere soothing won't do. I respect her reasons even when they are failing her, and this seems more than senility. It matters to her, and I don't know what she's *talking* about. So I chase all over the house until I find my mother. 'Amma, what is a *kurkut*?'

A niche set in the walls of an ancestral home, it turns out, where votive offerings are deposited and must be kept undisturbed if they are to prove their placation.

'And what was beyond the river?'

A village. A village whose powers of evil are so potent that nobody dares utter its name. It is referred to, under the breath, as Beyond-The-River instead.

One night we do all we can, and almost nothing helps. My mother, *garde-malade*, casts about for ways to make endurable what is clearly more than physical agony. 'Do you think you can try to keep your mind on your swami?'

'I can't,' Radhakka whispers. 'Because he is not there. There's no one there.'

Radhakka, Radhakka, you who taught me about telling stories of a sort, perhaps it would be kinder to you, to me, to all of us, if I told this as a story too, but I can't. This is not to patronize our story-telling past, not to disavow respect or need. For yes, after pain that formal feeling comes, and there can be a story . . . funny or sad, but uninjured by birth . . . that speaks of what happened.

As once you told me of twelfth-century Basavanna, whose songs and sayings you loved, maybe I can mention this century's Cocteau saying: 'Find out what you can do, and then do something else.' I don't want to resort to any practised ease of craft and fabrication to make you 'readable'. Just get our bare bones off the stove, and that perhaps sounds not only contradictory but too cannibalistic for comfort; but we have all been there, in one way or another, so why pretend and make pretty? I don't want a form of art, I want a form of life, to honour you as your own life never did.